ABOUT THE AUTHOR

Bridget is a novelist, prize winning short story writer and creative writing lecturer who has taught on undergraduate courses and in adult education. She has also been Writer in Residence at a community centre for the unemployed and a medical charity.

PRAISE FOR BACK TO CREATIVE WRITING SCHOOL

If you have any aspirations to pursue creative writing, this is an ideal book to help you keep focused. A must buy.
Ashley Lister, creative writing lecturer, Blackpool and the Fylde College

This book surprised and refreshed me in wonderful ways. I bought it hoping to learn a new trick or two for my teaching. But what I also found was that Whelan's sense of discovery revitalised my own writing. Working on fiction, after a decade as a poet, I had begun to see writing as a job; turning to this book after a particularly gruelling period of editing helped me to embark anew on the personal voyage writing always is for me at heart. One exercise triggered a sudden rush of character development for my third novel: a pivotal moment akin to falling in love.
Naomi Foyle, creative writing lecturer, Chichester University

Inspiring, insightful and fun – this easy-to-read guide explores what makes a good story and is packed with exercises to kick start your creativity. An indispensable tool for anyone wanting to write fiction, I highly recommend going back to school with Bridget.
Sarah Rayner, author of One Moment, One Morning, The Two Week Wait *and* Another Night, Another Day.

This fantastic, down to earth, imaginative and brilliantly organised programme of exercises and explanations will give enormous inspiration to anyone who has ever wondered about whether they could write. It is also full of great ideas for those of us with a little more experience behind us, and an invaluable resource for creative writing teachers. In other words, watch out, Bridget, I'm nicking your ideas...
Julia Crouch, author ~~of Cuckoo, Every Now You~~ Break, Tarnished and The Long Fall.

This is a power house of a book and Bridget Whelan's energy hums off the page. It is written with the authority of a creative writing tutor but also with warmth and an obvious love of her subject that makes writing seem easy, and writing well appear achievable. By presenting the exercises with an emphasis on play rather than work, Bridget encourages her readers to liberate their imagination. It's a great cure for writer's block!
Norma Curtis, former chair of the Romantic Novelists Association and author of Living it Up, Living it Down *and the* Tal and Ava *series.*

Bridget Whelan is an outstanding creative writing tutor and mentor, and teaches adults of all ages and abilities to kick start their creative writing talents. Having seen her classes first hand, I can recommend her as an amazing teacher. You won't be disappointed!
Susanna Quinn, author of The Glass Geisha, I Take this Woman, Show Don't Tell *and the* Ivy Lessons *series.*

From magical realism, to how to write funny, to horror, to crafting compelling description there's something for everyone in this fun and thought provoking creative writing book. Bridget has a lovely breezy, chatty style that makes it a real pleasure to read. Whether you're a novice or a published writer the exercises in this book will educate, inspire and delight you. Guaranteed to beat writers' block!
Cally Taylor, author of Heaven Can Wait, Home for Christmas *and* Secrets and Rain. *As CL Taylor, author of* The Accident.

If you want to get down to writing – or back to writing – but are struggling to get started, then this book is for you. Full of inspiring, stimulating exercises that will turn your writers' block into writers' flood – as your ideas pour onto the page! Bridget's warmth and experience shine on every page, it really feels as though you have the best kind of supportive teacher by your side, spurring you on and sharing her own wisdom. Recommended for new writers, and for old hands seeking new inspiration.
Kate Harrison, author of 14 fiction and non-fiction books, including The 5:2 Diet Book, The Secret Shopper's Revenge *and the* Soul Beach *trilogy for teenagers.*

Bridget Whelan

Back to
Creative
Writing
School

Cover design Simon Avery www.idobookcovers.com
Typesetting Ben Ottridge www.benottridge.co.uk

To Mike, always

ACKNOWLEDGEMENTS

There are many people to thank.

I want to acknowledge the 10+ years of active support and encouragement from writers Norma Curtis and Edward Milner with whom I have discussed every writing project and who saw an early draft and refrained from telling me to go away. I am very grateful to the generous, busy authors who took the time to read through a later draft and offered their comments

I owe a lot to the thoughtful work of proof readers Steve and Ben and the mistakes that remain are mine, all mine.

I also want to thank six women who haven't read this book yet and didn't know I was writing it, but helped all the same: Sue Smith, Julie Drake, Sheila McWattie, Judith Greenfield and my sister Eileen. And one who can't read yet, Aylah.

And I want to thank the students with whom I have worked. I have never left a classroom without learning something new about writing. I hope they can say the same.

CONTENTS

INTRODUCTION

This book is about writing.

About defeating the blank page. It's about taking risks and experimenting, giving yourself the freedom to make mistakes. It's about finding ideas and developing them.

Weaving stories in your head while you travel to work or sit daydreaming in a café is not writing. Something happens when you put words into the hard concrete of type or the softer clay of pen or pencil. You can start a sentence without knowing where it will end. You can bring unconnected ideas together and make something new. Working with your hand and head, you can discover what it is you want to write and it is *always* different to the way you thought it was going to be.

THIS BOOK WILL NOT TELL YOU HOW TO:

- write a bestseller at the weekend
- win competitions
- become rich and famous as a novelist.

Nor is it a guide to finding an agent or selling a short story. There are other books – good books – that can help with all that (except about being rich and famous, never trust a how-to book on that subject) and at the end I've listed some I know and like.

This book is about creating the material that might become a prizewinning short story or the novel you've always wanted to write.

It's about writing.

HOW TO USE THE BOOK

This book is laid out as if it was part of a course, but you don't need to follow it term by term. Dive in. The only advice I would give is finish each exercise you start. There are an awful lot of promising beginnings tucked away in dusty drawers and could-be novels stored in computers that are four chapters long. Don't add to the stockpile. Tenacity is part of a writer's job description and you will learn a lot just by finishing.

The best bit of writing advice I ever got was if you do something, something happens. Maybe tackling the exercises in this book will be part of your something – I hope so.

TERM ONE

PICK A NAME, ANY NAME

"The scariest moment is always just before you start"
Stephen King

This first exercise is very straightforward and it's about something that you're an expert in – you. All you have to do is list the names you've ever been called: the nice ones, the ones you answered to at different times in your life, the nicknames you've earned over the years, the variations of your proper name that have been used by family and friends and lisping toddlers.

In class I wouldn't ask you to include intimate names. While there's nothing wrong with the world knowing that someone calls you Dad or sweetheart, you don't need to declare to a room full of strangers that snuggle muffin was once whispered into your ear and you didn't mind a bit. Here, though, you are in control, write down as many names as you want, even the ones that might make others blush. This is your writing: you decide what to let go, what to hold back.

Work hard on the list and try to get to double figures. Jot down names you were called this week as well as the ones you haven't thought about since you were six. Think about the playground in the first school you ever attended, working out at a gym, nights spent clubbing. Think about the time you tasted your first kiss, attended your first job interview or played with your first child.

The only rule is that you have to write it down because something happens when you think with a pen in your hand. In this exercise what I am hoping will happen is that you will become a time traveller and visit a period of your life when you had different concerns and different priorities and sometimes answered to a different name.

Most of the exercises in this book focus on fiction writing – although many explore techniques that are equally useful in creative non-fiction. However, right at the beginning of your writing apprenticeship I think it makes sense to start with a short passage of autobiographical writing because it doesn't hurt to be reminded that:

1. You have never fitted under just one label.
2. There's nothing as interesting as people.
3. You can use your own life as a resource. You don't have to write your life story to use your experiences in a creative way. What you write in this exercise might develop into a theme for a novel or become the heart of a memoir. (Or it might simply be an exercise – you'll only know after you've written it.)

EXERCISE

Choose a name from your list and write a paragraph about it. A paragraph is a nicely imprecise length. Dickens could make one go on for pages. For most writers it is between two and six sentences... most of the time.

How does your name make you feel?
Do you hate it but somehow can't let go of it?
Do you like it and the side of your personality it represents?
Does it fit you? Did it ever?
If it is a nickname who is allowed to use it?

Write about the reason you were called this name – why your parents chose it or why friends fell into the habit of using it. If you aren't sure, speculate. Perhaps is a useful word in non-fiction. You aren't breaking faith with the reader and pretending to know something for certain when you don't, but it allows you to use your imagination to illuminate the shadows.

Something like this (perhaps)...

> *Perhaps Mum and Dad fought about it. He might have wanted something safe that was a nod to the sturdy farming roots he left behind when he came to the big city. Perhaps Mum was the edgy one who needed a wow! reaction when she presented me to the world. Perhaps there was a tug of war between Mary and Moonbeam, Hannah and Sapphire. Perhaps my name was chosen because neither of them actually hated it.*

Write your paragraph and if you find you have more to say, go on writing. I'll ask you to word count later, but right now write for as long as you have something to say. Write about the world where that name was first spoken. Write about the questions it throws up. And the answers you don't always have.

DESCRIPTION THAT MULTI TASKS

"Good description is never just description"
David Lodge

Descriptive passages have to justify their existence. If you think of a story as a journey, description forces the reader to stop. It's as if the author is saying hold on a moment, I know you want to find out what happens next, but I've created a whole new world for your enjoyment: there's the sun reflecting on the water and the girl's blond curls and the cold blue of a spring sky. Too much description and the reader might not bother to wait for the journey to start again. Too little and the reader might not care where the journey is heading.

You have to make a judgement about what to portray in words. If you look around where you are right now, reading these words, you can see a thousand things you could describe from the colour of the floor covering to the dust motes dancing in the air above your head. Shut your eyes. You can probably hear 20 sounds. Perhaps a motorcycle is revving outside and further away a young child is crying. Perhaps your chair creaks when you shift position.

If you tried to tell all of this to a reader the description could well grow to the size of a novella (that's about 20,000 to 50,000 words if you're wondering) and it would be deeply, deeply boring.

DESCRIPTION THAT MULTI TASKS

You are the reader's eyes and ears; you are their skin, their nostrils, their mouth. You can't tell everything so the few details you reveal have to reinforce the atmosphere of the story, or add to the development of a character, or contribute in some other way to the reader's understanding. For example, a red carpet could smack of fresh road kill or be as happy as a toddler's toy train. Whatever you choose the carpet is still red, but the words you use give it an added flavour that will stay with the reader and influence how they perceive the events that follow.

EXERCISE

Ok, let's tackle the place where you are at this moment. It doesn't matter if it is a cafe or your bedroom, this exercise will work wherever you are.

I want you to write a description of your surroundings in two distinct ways. Write in the first person for both passages: I said, I walked etc. However, you, the author, are not making the observations. The 'I' character is telling us what he or she sees and feels about the place you are in.

1) Describe where you are as if the 'I' character is revisiting a place where they were once held hostage.

Don't mention being imprisoned. This task is all about creating atmosphere. Study your surroundings. What would be important to someone desperate for a way out, but too scared to make an escape attempt? A prisoner must experience many emotions, including extreme tedium. Are there tiny details they would have noticed as they sat and waited while others controlled their lives? What would they still find disturbing about this place if they returned?

2) Describe this place as a sanctuary where the 'I' character once found shelter after being chased by a mob.

Again, don't mention anything about the mob. Instead concentrate on giving the impression that this was once a haven and is still somewhere where the 'I' character feels secure. You might choose the same details you used in the first exercise or you might decide that other features would be more important.

Remember you are writing about the same place, but in one it is a prison reeking of bad memories and in the other it is a refuge exuding a sense of safety. The grimy windows in the first description could have a gauze of dust in the second. You have your two themes: fear and peace. Your description has to evoke these sensations in the reader.

Write between 200 to 250 words for each descriptive passage. Do a word count and cut back if you've gone over. You don't want to overload the reader with a flood of images.

TITLE GAME

"Once you have a title you no longer have a blank page"
Kate Atkinson

The aim of this exercise is to come up with a quirky, intriguing title and use it as a diving board that you can launch from even though you don't know where you are going to land.

Bestselling novelist Kate Atkinson says that the title was all she had when she started to write many of her novels. You will find a list of Kate's books at the bottom of this section so, if you don't already know her work, you can see for yourself if she knows an attention-grabbing title when she sees one.

Titles are hard to get right. The easy option is to go for a label – *Sunday Afternoon, The Wedding, A Walk in the Park* and there's nothing intrinsically wrong in doing that. The problem is that it is unlikely to be memorable because you're treading a path that's already been well worn. Novelist and prize-winning short story writer Vanessa Gebbie suggests you Google your title and if numerous other stories pop up choose something more arresting. Vanessa has won major writing competitions and also been involved on the judging side (not at the same time).

LUCKY DIP EXERCISE

Choose a number between one and twelve.

1. rapid
2. immature
3. abundant
4. empty
5. harsh
6. crimson
7. countless
8. deafening
9. faint
10. ancient
11. smart
12. drowsy

Choose another number and you have another word, this time a noun.

1. days
2. love
3. lady
4. clouds
5. forest
6. nightmare
7. song
8. history
9. hands
10. riches
11. salt
12. eyes

This is your title. Go for it, even if the combination is odd, especially if the combination is odd. Sometimes it is the lucky accidents, the unexpected way two words rub against each other, that can set the imagination alight.

TITLE GAME

But if you want something that marches to a different drumbeat follow the example of the great science fiction writer Philip K. Dick who created titles such as:

Flow My Tears, the Policeman Said
The Man Whose Teeth Were All Exactly Alike
Do Androids Dream of Electric Sheep (made into the not-so-imaginatively-titled-film *Bladerunner*)

To add a potentially Philip K. Dick twist (the precise term is Dickian or Phildickian) to your title this time choose a number between 1 and 6 from the following selection of imposing literary phrases.

1) **Annihilating all that's made**
To a green thought in a green shade.
from *The Garden* by Andrew Marvell

2) **With flattering lips and with a double heart**
from Psalm 12

3) **And I watered it in fears,**
from *The Poison Tree* by William Blake

4) **I heard a fly buzz when I died**
from *Dying* by Emily Dickenson

5) **Freeze thou bitter sky**
from *Blow, blow thy winter wind* by William Shakespeare

6) **Millions on millions wait,**
from *A New National Anthem* by Shelley

So if you chose 1 and 1 you could have Rapid Days which I think has definite possibilities. Add another 1 in the spirit of Philip K. Dick and you might end up with something like:

Annihilating the rapid days

Or

Rapid days of green annihilation

(I've just checked and there is a satisfying nil Google entries for both phrases.)

Or you being you – and not me – would come up with something else entirely.

Start writing. Play with the ideas conjured up. Have fun. No word count, no direction, just see where the title will take you in half an hour. That's long enough to find out if the ideas aroused are substantial enough to hold your interest: if they are, carry on. If they aren't, choose another number.

Writers aren't always able to insist that their choice of title is the one used. In 1950 Isaac Asimov's short story about shape-changing aliens was accepted for publication. It was called *Green Patches*, but his editor changed it to *Misbegotten Missionary*. "Except for the alliteration, I can see no reason why this new title should appeal to any rational person," Asimov wrote later. He waited 18 years before grabbing the chance to publish it under its original title when his short story collection *Nightfall One* appeared. However, I'm pretty sure Kate Atkinson was responsible for these titles.

Behind the Scenes at the Museum (1995)
Human Croquet (1997)
Emotionally Weird (2000)
Not the End of the World (2002) short story collection
Case Histories (2004)
One Good Turn (2006)
When Will There Be Good News? (2008)
Started Early, Took My Dog (2010)
Life After Life (2013)

BECOME A
CLICHÉ KILLER

"The most original authors are not so because they advance what is new, but because they put what they have to say as if it had never been said before"
Johann Wolfgang von Goethe

A cliché doesn't start life worn out. On the contrary, when the ink was fresh it created such vivid pictures in the mind of the reader that it was used again and again and again.

And then it died

Or almost. It retains just enough life to creep into your writing without you noticing. There you are, typing away, convinced that you've drawn an emotionally evocative portrait of the love between a father and son only to find when you read it again that the son is the apple of Dad's eye, a phrase that's been knocking around since the Dark Ages – literally. There is a record of the Saxon King Alfred the Great using it in the 9th century and it probably wasn't new then. There's no shame in discovering a cliché in your first draft, but hang your head if you allow it to survive. Put it out of its misery and press delete. Better still work out exactly what you wanted the reader to feel and find your own words to express that thought.

That's what this exercise is all about, but first you need a good working definition so you can spot a cliché slinking near the keyboard. I don't think you can better George Orwell on the subject.

Never use a metaphor, simile, or other figure of speech which you are used to seeing in print.

It's a high standard and you're going to fall below it sometimes, but it is the kind of challenge that will make you the best writer you can be.

I would add a qualification, however, and I don't think the great man would mind. It's usually ok to use a cliché in dialogue because that is an accurate reflection of the way people talk (but you don't want dialogue to be too natural – more on that later.) A novel full of characters who always spoke in sparklingly original phrases might be a little hard to believe.

And another qualification – especially for anyone who learnt English as a second language – there's a good chance that clichés in your first language are inventive and intriguing in English. I discovered that when talking with Lijia Zhang, the Chinese journalist and author. In English the irritating little lines that appear around your eyes if you lived long enough and laughed hard enough are called crow's feet. In Chinese they are fish tails.

A few more definitions might be useful before starting the exercise.

A metaphor is a commanding figure of speech. It makes connections between things that are different, except in one particular way, and says that the connection is so strong, so overwhelming, that the two things meld together.

The truck driver *was a* bear.
Your room *is a* pigsty.

A simile is exactly the same, but quieter and with better manners. It's pointing out the similarity between two things that initially seem so unalike. However, it's not suggesting that there has been a transformation.

That man *is like* a bear.
Your room *is like* a pigsty.

EXERCISE

The task is to rewrite a few familiar (and therefore clichéd) figures of speech. For example, instead of the almost meaningless phrase as white as a ghost you could have as white as uncooked pastry or as white as milk left out overnight ...it's the kind of thing you could puzzle over when you are stuck in traffic or on a train journey: being a writer means never being bored again.

Is it worth the effort?

The main character in the opening pages of Cormac McCarthy's post-apocalyptic novel *The Road* remembers the nightmare that troubled him the previous night:

> ...*the creature raised its dripping mouth from the rimstone pool and stared into the light with eyes white and sightless as the eggs of spiders.*

I hope that's enough to convince you that it is worth a lot of effort.

Here are a couple of similes that need to be put out of their misery.

She was as brave as a lion.
They fought like cat and dog.

And here are two flabby, cringe-worthy metaphors that need a lot more punch.

The world is my oyster.
The sound was music to his ears.

However, it is hard to come up with something striking and original without a context, so here are a bagful of mini stories to wrap around each of these clichés – do them all if you can.

She was as brave as a lion
A child facing playground bullies
A student fighting off a rapist
An old woman taking the hand of her vampire grandson

They fought like cat and dog
Squabbling teenage brothers
Married ghosts still bickering in the afterlife,
Police officers, hungry for promotion, investigating a crime

The world is my oyster
A graduate with his examination results in his hand
A lottery winner
Young person on his or her first holiday without Mum and Dad

The sound was music to his ears
Dad listening to his unborn child's heartbeat
A country and western singer savouring the audience's rapturous response
A murderer nailing down the lid of a homemade coffin....

INVENTING PEOPLE

"It begins with a character, usually, and once he stands up on his feet and begins to move, all I can do is trot along behind him with a paper and pencil trying to keep up long enough to put down what he says and does"
William Faulkner

Writers play God. Editing, cutting, spell checking, double checking grammar, polishing sentences is the hard work: this is the fun bit. Maybe this is why we write. We get to make people up and then – in the words of Stephen King – we throw stones at them to see what happens and if we are lucky our characters start throwing the stones around in ways we never anticipated.

In *A Good Confession* my main character's mother got to do pretty much what she wanted. If I got stuck I'd send her in and she would put everyone on edge and mess things up nicely.

Readers meet her for the first time in this scene when her daughter Cathleen reveals that her husband is seriously ill:

oOo

'Jaysus! His liver?'
Cathleen nodded. Her mother's voice was rising in pitch and volume.
'Good God, has that man of yours been keeping secrets?'

'What?' Cathleen's head jerked up. She had crawled into an armchair after returning from the hospital: it was the first night she and Mick had spent apart since they married.
'Isn't it amazing what a smile can hide. Did you never suspect? Or have you been hiding it from us too?' Kitty demanded.
'I'm hiding nothing.' Cathleen spoke without emotion. 'Mick's never had the money to ruin his liver.'
'They're all liars, men. Do you know how much he earns? You don't! And if he said, you couldn't believe him. Ach, they're all cheats.'
'It's an infection,' said Cathleen as if her mother hadn't spoken. 'An abscess caused by infection. The doctor explained.'
Kitty, moving to and fro in the Brogan's sitting room, bumped into the heavy mahogany dining table that stood in the centre, nearly knocking over a standard lamp.
'Infection? Is that what they're calling it? Men covering up for one another, that's what that is.'

oOo

When I set out to write a novel about two people breaking the rules of their culture and their religion, I never suspected that Kitty, with her bony elbows and heavy eyebrows, would be the character I would fall in love with...My publicist wanted me to write a prequel of Kitty's life, exploring what made her the interfering and lion-hearted woman she became. Perhaps I'll get around to it one day.

This character creation exercise is in three parts. First, a bit of fun that will help you find the right name for a character that doesn't exist right now, but will live and breathe and fight and love by the time you come to the end of the exercise. Then an opportunity to dig deep, burrowing under the skin of the character because if you truly believe in him or her, they will walk off the page straight into the reader's imagination and finally, an action scene to discover what they are made of.

NAMING EXERCISE
The raw material is the letters of your own name but don't even try to make an anagram. That's a time wasting diversion that will take you from the real business of writing, just play around with them...

INVENTING PEOPLE

To illustrate what I mean, I'll show you what I've done with my name: Bridget Margaret Whelan

Here's what I came up with:

- Greta
- Alan
- Garrett
- Lard

Ok – Greta Garrett is memorable

I like all those Grr-rr sounds. It makes a kind of entrance. GG could be the editor of a magazine, a politician, a hero in her own life. I'm not entirely sure I would go out for a drink with her (or if she would ask me), but I like her already.

Alan is one of those names that doesn't reveal much, but put it in front of the faintly amusing Lard and you have someone reminiscent of the 1940s actor Alan Ladd, star of classic black and white movies including the iconic cowboy film *Shane* where he really did ride off into the sunset. Maybe that suggests some characteristics: a nearly man, a man who is slightly ridiculous, slightly sad... and lard means animal fat so weight could be a problem.

I also came up with some nicknames. They don't have to make sense: some of the most enduring nicknames are created through a chance misunderstanding or childish mispronunciation and over time they become part of a family's vocabulary.

- Retta
- Whee
- Marl

How about Whee Garrett?

Now that's different. You haven't met her before, have you?

Work on your own name and come up with a man and a woman. You will need two characters for the next exercise so start working on them now. Make the names distinctive, names that stand out in a crowd.

Write them down. Put circles around them. Congratulations, you've just given birth.

Before moving onto the next exercise, I want to say a little more about the naming of characters. Sometimes your character has a real life source and grows out of the people you love and the people you hate. John Grisham, writer of bestselling legal thrillers, says that one of the reasons he writes is that it is a good way of getting his own back. Fine. There's no doubt that a bullying boss, a sanctimonious acquaintance or the teacher with a vicious tongue are all good material, but if you are going to plunder your own life avoid the law courts.

LEGAL ACTION

If your character is based on a flesh and blood person at the very least make sure the fictional name is radically different to their real life one. That includes the good guys. Legal action was taken against Kathryn Stockett, author of *The Help,* by a maid working for a family member who had a name similar to the main character. Now in this instance the author denied any connection between the two and the case was dismissed, but be aware that even if you create a sympathetic hero the real life counterpart might not be happy. Better that Marianne becomes Bertha than she morphs into a Marilyn.

The next piece of advice may sound trivial, but names in a story should not start with the same letter. I know they do in real life, but you want the reader to be able to distinguish between the characters without giving it much thought. Imagine a short story about three friends: Emma, Sally and Sarah. I would bet good money that the reader is going to mix up the two S's at some point and that could very well be the point they put the story down. You can do a lot of things, take a lot of risks, but don't ever confuse readers unless you want them to be confused, as in *One Hundred Years of Solitude* where most of the men have the same or similar names.

Names reflect the fashion of the time. Your story will lose all credibility if you cast Tiffany as a Welsh land army girl in World War II. There are many internet sites that will help you avoid that kind of mistake. Here are two that I've found.

A section of the USA Social Security Administration website is devoted to the most popular male and female names in America over the last 100 years. You can find it here: http://www.ssa.gov/oact/babynames/top5names.html. This is fascinating stuff: Jennifer topped the polls from 1970 to 1984 while Michael was in the top two boy's names from 1954 until 2008. It also lists the most popular 100 names state by state in the last 50 years. You don't necessarily want to go with the most popular – it might be better to pick names that were less common but you know were in currency at the time of your story, so you can achieve the right period flavour.

In 1960, for instance, David and Mary were the most popular name across the USA while Barry and Joanne were the 100th most popular names in Illinois. They would make a good couple as would Ernest and Evelyn from Georgia. This is an example where names beginning with the same letter might just work. (Never stick to any rule if there is a good reason to break it.)

British Baby Names – Trends, Styles and Quirks is an engaging if rather eccentric website that has a database going back to the 1880s. http://www.britishbabynames.com From this source I learned that David and Susan were the most popular names in 1964 while the 100th most popular girl's name was Stephanie with Dominic for the boys. I can see Steff and Dom grooving to Wham! when they were in their twenties and worrying about the economy now that retirement isn't so far away.

RESEARCH WARNING

I should add a warning here. Research is seductive, giving you the feeling that you are working even though not a line has been added to your story. You could while away a whole afternoon selecting the right names and still not have invented a character. So, let's get on with the exercise that will help you do just that. By the time you finish you will have a whole person. In fact, you will have two whole people (you chose a male and female remember) with their own special talents and habits and neuroses that make them like no other person that has ever lived.

Unique. Believable. Alive.

INTERVIEW EXERCISE

This questionnaire is adapted from one developed by the late 19th century French writer Marcel Proust (author of *Remembrance of Things Past*) and is my version of a traditional creative writing tool. It will reveal things about your characters that you will never ever use, but the more you know about them the more believable they will become. You can use it as we are doing here, to create new characters from scratch, but it is also helpful when you are in the middle of a story. Getting re-acquainted with your central characters and discovering new things about them will get the story moving again if it has started to sag.

You can answer as the all-knowing author, but I think it is more interesting to borrow the hot seat technique from the acting profession. In class students would each take it in turn to answer random questions 'in character'. In a similar way, you can create new fictions by answering my questionnaire in your character's voice, but he or she might avoid certain lines of enquiry. Sometimes the thing that isn't said can reveal more than copious amounts of information. Here's an extract from an interview to show you what I mean.

WHEE GARRETT

Q. If you were in a bar what drink would you order?

A. Oh, come on! Why on earth would you want to know that? I don't know. An orange juice? A coffee? Do they have anything as civilized as that? I don't mind having a glass of wine with a meal if it's a special occasion, but a bar? You must be able to think of a better question than that...

Was a parent an alcoholic? An ex-husband? Perhaps she is a secret drinker herself and the glass-of-wine-with-dinner approach screens a dark tragedy. Or maybe she has deep-seated religious beliefs that influence her reaction to the question. Only Whee and I know the answer and I'd only reveal it if it helped the story she appeared in.

QUESTIONAIRE – use it for both characters

Avoid one word answers unless that is part of your character's personality. Everything your character says will help you to uncover elements of their temperament.

- What is your most treasured possession?
- What is your favourite journey?
- When and where were you happiest?
- When did you last cry?
- What is your greatest extravagance?
- What is your greatest regret?
- Which talent would you most like to have?
- If you were in a bar what drink would you order?
- What is the trait you most deplore in yourself?
- What is the trait you most deplore in others?
- Which words or phrases do you most overuse?
- If you could change one thing about yourself, what would it be?
- What's the one thing you wouldn't want anyone else to know about you?

To my mind the most interesting question out of all of them is the last. The answer to that could even lead you into a story.

I once set this exercise when I took over a class of first time novelists at short notice. When we shared the results I realised one writer was having serious problems. He revealed that his central character's response to the last question was *I don't want anyone to know I'm a jerk*.

No one thinks they are a jerk.

They may be a jerk, but inside their head they are just fine. Or if their self-esteem is low, jerk is too mild a word.

Think about the mental landscape of a bully. Very few think they are a bully. They would justify their behaviour to themselves and to the outside world by saying things like: I was only having a bit of fun. I was doing her a favour. He has to learn to man up. You've got to be tough to survive. She can't take a joke. I've had a lot worse said to me...

British film director Mike Leigh is famous for wanting his actors to have such an intimate knowledge of the character they are playing that they should all – including those with a non-speaking part – know how they celebrated their eighth birthday. It will never come out in a film, but if the actor is inside the character's head they will act out of instinct and that's how we should write.

CONFLICT EXERCISE

Now you have created a man and a woman, decide which one you like best. Which one would you prefer to meet in real life? Label that one character A.

Your task is to bring the two characters together. Perhaps they are sister and brother, father and daughter, mother and son, young lovers, or married for 30 years. Or it could be that they just happen to be next to each other in a queue or sitting opposite each other on a train.

Perhaps they work together...perhaps one is the doctor and one is the patient, one is the plumber and the other the householder, a counsellor and client, students on the same course, drug dealer and police officer...

Once you've thought of the connection you can set up the scene. Character A tries to persuade the other character to commit a deed that you *personally* feel to be morally wrong. It could be a small thing – not paying the right bus fare. It could be a huge thing: it could be murder. You probably won't like me very much for putting the characters you have just created in this difficult position, but we get to know what someone is made of when they are faced with a challenge.

Good people do bad things sometimes: bad people can have genuine warmth and charm. I'm hoping that this exercise will produce someone you could imagine having an argument with; someone you would bother to argue with rather than dismiss as irredeemably awful. That's why I've asked you choose an action that you feel is straight-down-the-middle, black and white wrong. It should add depth to the writing.

And working out character A's motives could give you a story. In what circumstances would he or she be willing to kill another person, steal, cheat, or lie? To find that out maybe you have to ask yourself in what circumstances would you be willing to kill another person, steal, cheat or lie.

It's a tough exercise, no doubt about that, and an important one because characters are important. It's why I read. It's why I write. Don't worry about getting it wrong. You almost certainly will. Ernest Hemmingway, in his blunt, manly way said that the first draft of anything is shit. There's a freedom in that thought. Don't demand perfection from yourself, at least not first time. Be prepared to come back to this scene and rewrite it later.

How long should it be?

The key word in the instructions is *persuade* and that takes time. You also want to reveal what these two people are like. We spend a lifetime getting to know those around us so your characters shouldn't reveal every aspect of their personality within a few pages, as if they were manufactured in a factory with loving mother or jealous lover stamped across their foreheads. So, the scene should be as long as it has to be to do the job, although I can't imagine it would be over 1000 words. The final version could be a lot shorter.

You've already done a lot of work on creating your characters now is the time to see them in action. End the scene when character B agrees or refuses. By then they are both going to have real blood moving through their veins.

THE HISTORY OF A HOUSE

"Writing is like sculpturing words out of a block of imagination. Sentences chisel the story, then characters make it their own"

Federico Chini

This is my version of a property advert of the kind you can read in many magazines. It's a patchwork of phrases I've taken from a variety of sources.

A charming house on the XXXXX borders offers wonderful family accommodation and four pretty acres of gardens

The property dates in its present form from the 18th century, but it is believed to have burnt down the century before, leaving only the mellowed stone shell for later generations to embellish. No sign of that historic crisis now exists and the character-filled house features exposed beams, stone floors and impressive fireplaces – one with an ancient bread oven exposed giving an enchanting period feel.

Recently refurbished, the kitchen/breakfast room boasts an oil-fired Aga and double Belfast sink and there are three further reception rooms. The five bedrooms are spread over two floors upstairs and all have delightful views.

The converted barn is now a romantic studio apartment with a heart-shaped bath. There is also an old wash house which has an unusual first floor greenhouse with rare glass pantiles. The inviting walled garden to the rear has a magnificent maze.

EXERCISE

Your task is to put people in this house.

They can be living there now or at some other point in its 200+ year history. Perhaps there are occasions when it has been overcrowded, derelict, a happy home, the spooky house of the neighbourhood, owned by a miser, by a slave trader, by a wealthy young couple addicted to lavish parties, perhaps it was the headquarters of a gang of highwaymen, perhaps it was a celebrity's hideaway, perhaps the servants taking care of the house were a lot more interesting than those who owned it... Who started the fire and made the maze? Who wanted a greenhouse overlooking the garden and liked to decorate with heart shapes?

Don't do any research just yet...

Wait until you're sure you have a story worth researching. Confine the action to the house and grounds and work at getting under the skin of your character. A miser in 1780 (when the American War of Independence was raging and Anti-Catholic rioters were causing trouble in London) might well have many of the same concerns as a miser in 1980 (when John Lennon was murdered in New York and UK inflation was just under 22%).

Put people in the house doing something, feeling something, and later you can put the right kind of clothes on their back, have them sitting in the right kind of chair at the dinner table and eating the right kind of food. In the first draft let the house and the characters meld together and work some magic.

THE I-DON'T-WANT-TO-WRITE-A-POEM POETRY EXERCISE

"Most people ignore most poetry because most poetry ignores most people"

Adrian Mitchell

I see the same delighted/horrified expressions in class at the start of every term when students see that poetry is included in the list of subjects I have lined up for them.

This exercise is for the scared, for those who have an urgent need to try another exercise, any exercise, rather than write a poem. You're in safe hands, I'm not a poet.

I think that makes me just about perfect for this task. After all, if you were taking your first tentative steps with word processing you wouldn't want to face Bill Gates across the table, would you?

Three good reasons why someone who will never ever write a poem of their own free will should do this exercise:

1.   It makes you think about using language with precision.

2. It is a challenge but it is a do-able challenge. Poetry is about rules and the rules for this first exercise are so simple and straightforward seven year olds can understand them. In fact seven year olds do this kind of poetry all the time. That doesn't make it childish or easy – doing the best you can is never easy.
3. At the end you'll have written a poem. Hey!

Three good reasons why someone who writes poetry should do this exercise:

It's a gentle stretch of your poetic muscles, a limbering up.
It might push you in new directions.
At the end you'll have written a poem. Hey!

An acrostic is a passage of writing where the initial letter spells out a word or phrase. Starting life as a way of revealing prophecies in ancient Greece, it has been popular with readers of the New York Times as an intellectual word game for over half a century and is sometimes described as being halfway between crosswords and sudoko.

Acrostics have been messages of hope when times are dangerous and the most famous example is the acrostic used by early Christians. The words Jesus Christ, God's Son, Saviour spelt out fish in Greek, which is why it became a symbol for a persecuted community. It has also been a way of delivering instructions to spies and insults to those you hate. A classic Anglo Saxon insult was engraved in an acrostic epithet on a Montréal headstone in the 1990s, said to have been ordered by an ex-wife joining forces with an ex-lover.

And it can be a poem.

The important thing to remember about any poem is that it is an oral art form. That means how words sound together matter. For this exercise all you need worry about is selecting the right word to start each line and reading it aloud often to check that it flows well. Reading aloud is a good idea for any piece of writing – at the editing stage it can even help with punctuation – but is essential for poetry.

EXERCISE

Name acrostics have always been popular and the content has to relate to the person in some way. Here's the one that appears at the end of *Alice Through the Looking Glass*. Lewis Carroll spelt out Alice Liddell's full name, the child to whom he dedicated the book.

A boat beneath a sunny sky,
Lingering onward dreamily
In an evening of July--

Children three that nestle near,
Eager eye and willing ear,
Pleased a simple tale to hear--

Long has paled that sunny sky:
Echoes fade and memories die.
Autumn frosts have slain July.

Still she haunts me, phantomwise,
Alice moving under skies
Never seen by waking eyes.

Children yet, the tale to hear,
Eager eye and willing ear,
Lovingly shall nestle near.

In a Wonderland they lie,
Dreaming as the days go by,
Dreaming as the summers die:

Ever drifting down the stream--
Lingering in the golden gleam--
Life, what is it but a dream?

Your own acrostic doesn't have to be as long as this, but the more complex the poem the more subtle and hidden the acrostic becomes.

Go back to the very first exercise and choose one of the names you wrote down. Don't choose the shortest name you've ever been called or the one with the easiest letters, go for the one you like the best. If that means bending the rules, bend them and make it yours. For example, Edgar Allen Poe wrote a love poem to a girl called Elizabeth and got around the awkward Z by amending the name of Socrates' wife Xanthippe and calling her Zantippe instead. I was going to put the whole poem here for you to see what he had done, but I have to be honest and say it's rather dreary. I much prefer his stories. Look it up if you're interested and one thing to take from it is that there's nothing as elastic as a writer's imagination.

In the simplest acrostic you can have one word per line as in this ancient example written by that most prolific of writers – anon.

Devoted,
On
Guard

This is my attempt at something a bit longer.

Bashful like one of the seven dwarves
Reserved like a table
In a restaurant
Dream heavy like all writers should be
Greedy for that thing called
Education wanting to...
Teach and be taught

Give it a go and don't forget to read it aloud. Change it until you are pleased with the way the words sound together.

There! You have a poem. This could even be the way you sign your emails from now on....

THE TASTE OF A PLACE AND OH, HOW IT SMELLS

"Good writing is supposed to evoke sensation in the reader – not the fact that it is raining, but the feeling of being rained upon"

E.L. Doctorow

We are visual people. Most of us think in pictures most of the time, which is why description usually focuses on how something or someone looks. However, by introducing at least one of the other senses – sound, smell, taste, touch – you can add a depth to your writing that allows the reader to move from being a passive observer to being part of an imaginative experience.

The mantra of any creative writing course is show don't tell. I think the following examples demonstrate why.

Tell
The man stumbling along the narrow lane was a tramp wearing torn old clothes that didn't fit him properly and hadn't been washed in weeks.

A bit of 'Show'
The man's shirt was torn and his dirty jeans were trailing in the dust as he stumbled along the narrow lane.

And a bit more

The man's shirt was torn and the spiky smell of old urine clung to jeans that trailed in the dust as he stumbled along the narrow lane.

Ok, so it works for fiction, but something else happens when you want to write about an event from your own life. Concentrating on the senses helps you to go back in time. The mental image you have of Aunt Aggie's face may have dimmed over the years, but if you can remember what her kitchen smelt like on Sunday mornings then you are back there, drawing pictures in the steam on her window.

This is how Proust put it:

> *...the greater part of our memory exists outside us, in a dampish breeze, in the musty air of a bedroom or the smell of autumn' s first fires ... the last vestige of the past, the best part of it, the part which, after all our tears seem to have dried can make us weep again.*

There's a problem though. Scientists say that we can recognise up to 10,000 separate smells. Our noses are bombarded with information from food, animals, earth, plants, bacterial decomposition, industrial processes, and other people and yet we don't have a large vocabulary to describe how something smells. And it is very, very hard to describe a smell to someone who has not already experienced it.

The same is true for taste. Smell and taste are linked together because back in the dawn of time the two senses had the same purpose: to guide our ancestors towards stuff that might be good to eat and away from something that could be harmful. Most of the flavour of food comes from its smell, which floats up to cells in the nose through the nostrils and also through a passageway at the back of the mouth. Food is dull when we can't smell it – it's no more than fuel.

EXERCISE

In this exercise I want to work with both taste and smell, but you may find one is more powerful than the other in which case go with that one. This is a tough exercise. To make it easier I want you to use sensory description to describe a place that you already know. I've given you a list of three places, choose the one you want to write about or really challenge yourself and do all three. Be specific. Think of an office that you have a strong memory of – not some general, generic office or one you've seen on television – but one where you've spent time. It should be somewhere you can see in colour when you close your eyes.

Choose one of these:

1.   An office
2.   A bedroom
3.   A car

Ok, you're now going to step into the picture.

As quick as you can, write down five things you ate or tasted in that place. For example a sandwich or the glue on the back of a stamp.

Next note down five smells you associate with that place – it can have something to do with one of the tastes you've just jotted down or something else entirely, such as lavender air freshener or socks taken off the night before.

Try to do five for each. It's a stretch because I've avoided places that fill our senses such as kitchens and gardens. I want it to be first-hand experience, particular to you and that place, not borrowed from a shared understanding of what kitchens should smell like.

Now you should have 10 words or phrases. Work on the one or two that brings that place back to life for you. Perhaps you were always chewing gum when you got out of school and climbed into the car. Perhaps the smell of the road outside drifted through the open window in the summer.

Put that taste and smell into a paragraph. Be precise in the detail. Not just chewing gum but also the flavour and even the make if you can remember it. Re-introduce visual elements. Re-create the place as it existed in that particular period of your life.

Now write around it. What were you doing back then? Where were you living? Who was your best friend? Write and don't think about word counting. See what comes out.

ALLITERATION: WINNING WORDS, SMART SENTENCES

"The difference between the right word and the almost right word is the difference between lightning and a lightning bug"

Mark Twain

This is a poetic device that shouldn't be left to poets because it can also produce interesting affects in prose. The writer only has the words on a page. There's no background soundtrack or swelling orchestral climax to build mood, no slow-panned close up to underline the emotional atmosphere. Alliteration can allow the reader to stand at your shoulder hearing what you want her to hear, seeing what you want him to see.

Use with caution though – think of it as seasoning. Don't be heavy handed.

It's a very simple device that very young children enjoy long before they can read. All you have to do is start as many words as you can in a phrase with the same sound. (Not the same letter – this is not about how it looks on the page, but how it sounds in your head when you read it. That means K and C go together when they produce that Kerrr sound and W and R as in write and right.)

Tongue twisters are alliterative as in the famous old standby

Peter Piper picked a peck of pickled peppers.
A peck of pickles Peter Piper picked.
If Peter Piper picked a peck of pickled peppers,
How many pickled peppers did Peter Piper pick?

It's worth having a go at something similar for the sheer fun and energy of it. It is also a reminder that lots of fictional characters have names that start with the same sound: Mickey Mouse, Peter Parker (aka Spiderman), Sam Spade

I first came across the next tongue twister in a workshop to prepare writers reading aloud in public for the first time. It shows that alliteration can produce subtle textures.

Three grey geese in a green field grazing,
Grey were the geese and green was the grazing.

Here's a few more examples:

From Shakespeare's *The Tempest*

Full fathom five thy father lives

And there is an extremely generous amount of ds in these lines from *The Windhover* by the Victorian poet Father Gerard Manley Hopkins:

kingdom of daylight' s dauphin, dapple-dawn-drawn Falcon

That's five in a row – six if you count the dom of kingdom, which I think you should as its stressed. Read it aloud and you'll see what I mean. I am not keen on dapple-dawn-drawn because it's such hard work for the reader without much benefit – rather too much chilli in the con carne for my taste, but you might like it.

For me, there is something much more interesting going on in *Anthem for Doomed Youth* by World War I poet Wilfred Owen.

> *What passing-bells for these who die as cattle?*
> > *Only the monstrous anger of the guns.*
> > *Only the stuttering rifles' rapid rattle*
> *Can patter out their hasty orisons.*
> *No mockeries now for them; no prayers nor bells,*
> > *Nor any voice of mourning save the choirs, —*
> *The shrill, demented choirs of wailing shells;*
> > *And bugles calling for them from sad shires.*

In the third line the alliterative phrase **stuttering rifles' rapid rattle** produces something like the sound of gunfire not only by choosing words beginning with r, but also through the double tts of stutter and rattle. (So technically this is also onomatopoeia when the words spoken aloud make the sound of the thing they are describing.) A quieter, more restrained anger is introduced at the end of the stanza with the phrase sad shires.

Owen also used alliteration in the very last line of this poem.

> *And each slow dusk a drawing-down of blinds.*

To me that represents the loss that endures across decades even when it isn't spoken aloud, the loss of the young men destroyed in the trenches and the loss of the children that they never had. Owen himself was part of that lost generation. He was killed at the age of 25 seven days before the Armistice was signed in November 1918.

PROSE EXERCISE
1) To start this task all you need do is write your own absurd sentence or tongue twister. Be as inventive as you can while still making sense and obeying the usual rules of English. Here's my not exactly brilliant example. I'm sure you can do much better.

> *Bridget's breakfasts of burnt bread and beige beverages were a bleak beginning to the business of the day.*

(It's not that bad at my house, but dinners are probably better...)

2) Now you get serious. Play with sound and write a couple of sentences that you could imagine using in a short story or novel. Here's my attempt:

My mother mumbles a memory from our shared past, makes a mistake, moves on, makes another and mouths a moist apology

I think we can all probably agree that I've grown a little too fond of Ms here, but there is an underlying sadness that is connected to the sound of the words as well as their meaning. A little pruning would do no harm, but alliteration has added to the emotional meaning.

Play around with different letters and write two or three sentences about

1. Two people having an argument
2. A lost child
3. A violent storm

POETRY EXERCISE

As we've seen alliteration is an oral device, concerned with how words sound so this is a perfect opportunity to think about writing a poem.

Give yourself five minutes to jot down phrases stuffed with alliteration. Write quickly. This is top of the head stuff. Throw them out onto the page without worrying if they are any good. You can make a judgement when your five minutes is up. Choose two you like and tidy them up a bit.

Here's a couple I came up with:

The setting sun shone on the southern slopes.

A grey cat growled stalking shadows in the long grass

ALLITERATION: WINNING WORDS, SMART SENTENCES

Forgetting about alliteration for the moment, force yourself to see that setting sun (or whatever you've got).

Start asking questions: the southern slopes of what? A French hill purple with lavender, a ski resort in February, a rubbish mountain of car carcases?

Search for the picture that you want the reader to see. The sun's colour was like what? An orange? A fire? Maybe a dying fire because the sun is about to set, but is that dangerously close to being a cliché? Is a fading fire better?

Use at least one of these images. Put the alliteration back. Add some more phrases that make sense of that image and put it in context. Stir well. Come back the next day (or next week) and see if you like the result. If you do it's a poem, if you don't it's practice.

MUSIC IN WORDS

"Words have music and if you are a musician you will write to hear them"

E.L. Doctorow

Music can enter your writing through the words you choose if you write with your ear as well as your hand. John McGahern, the Irish writer, wrote his memoir after he was diagnosed with cancer.

Here's an extract:

> *Heaven was in the sky. My mother spoke to me of heaven as concretely and with as much love as she named the wild flowers. Above us the sun of heaven shone. Beyond the sun was the gate of heaven.*

There's rhythm in this passage created by the author's careful selection of words, his use of repetition and the way he varies the length of the sentences. The result is very simple and very beautiful. McGahern may well have been influenced by the kind of traditional music he would have heard all his life. Here it is described by John B Keane in *The Bodhran Makers*.

> *Beating out the age-old timbre of the bodhran, thunderous when demanded, gentle and muted too as a solitary concertina player rendered a tune... coaxed the delicate note, teased the*

long note, jerked the short and wrestled the powerful from the insignificant instrument...

There's an altogether different tempo playing in this description of Los Angeles in Martin Amis' *Money*.

You walk left, you walk right, you are a bank rat on a busy river. This restaurant serves no drink, this one serves no meat, this one serves no heterosexuals. You can get your chimp shampooed, you can get your dick tattooed, twenty-four hour, but can you get lunch?

What is it: modern jazz, punk? I'm thinking more along the lines of a perspiring Jacques Brel with a glass in his hand.

Music can enter your writing through the story you want to tell. The short story that some critics have called the best ever written is James Joyce's *The Dead*, from his collection *Dubliners*. Indeed when I was studying for a Masters in Creative Writing a tutor apologised for giving it as a set text as he feared that we might lose heart and put down our pens.

The main character is Gabriel, a middle aged man attending his family's annual Christmas party in Dublin in 1906. As in previous years speeches are made, dances are danced, meals ate and the same embarrassing relative gets drunk.

Here's an extract from the beginning.

A light fringe of snow lay like a cape on the shoulders of his overcoat and like toecaps on the toes of his goloshes; and, as the buttons of his overcoat slipped with a squeaking noise through the snow-stiffened frieze, a cold, fragrant air from out-of-doors escaped from crevices and folds.
"Is it snowing again, Mr. Conroy?" asked Lily.
She had preceded him into the pantry to help him off with his overcoat. Gabriel smiled at the three syllables she had given his surname and glanced at her. She was a slim; growing girl, pale in complexion and with hay-coloured hair. The gas in the pantry

made her look still paler. Gabriel had known her when she was a child and used to sit on the lowest step nursing a rag doll.

"Yes, Lily," he answered, "and I think we're in for a night of it."
He looked up at the pantry ceiling, which was shaking with the stamping and shuffling of feet on the floor above, listened for a moment to the piano and then glanced at the girl, who was folding his overcoat carefully at the end of a shelf.

"Tell me. Lily," he said in a friendly tone, "do you still go to school?"

"O no, sir," she answered. "I'm done schooling this year and more."

"O, then," said Gabriel gaily, "I suppose we'll be going to your wedding one of these fine days with your young man, eh? "
The girl glanced back at him over her shoulder and said with great bitterness:
"The men that is now is only all palaver and what they can get out of you."

If you don't already know the story, I'm hoping that this is enough to give you a taste of Joyce's writing, but it is probably not enough to help you understand why so many hold it in such high regard. I suppose the short answer is that it works: the reader has a sense of being there, that real people are shaking off the snow and dancing and talking.

Having said that, stories are about something happening and what happens in this story is that Gabriel's wife is deeply moved by a song sung at the party. That's it.

No dramatic scene to disturb this middle class and middle aged community. Later when they are alone she explains to her husband that she was reminded of a boy who was in love with her when she was growing up in Galway and who, already ill, waited outside her window in the cold. He died as a result.

After she falls asleep, Gabriel reflects on his own life and what his wife has said. It is snowing again and he imagines it falling as a blanket over Ireland and over the grave of the young boy. Joyce lets us into his character's heart but he doesn't interpret or explain. We can feel Gabriel's emptiness and understand that he is left questioning everything he has achieved. One of the reasons we can accept this epiphany is that music was the means of unlocking memories and giving new life to emotions that were submerged. It's powerful stuff.

The Japanese author Haruki Murakami uses music in a similar way to evocate a time, a place, a mood. In his international bestseller novel *Norwegian Wood*, the central character hears the Beatles song by chance and is thrust back 20 years to his student days in Tokyo.

Music can also be a way of developing character. Ian Rankin's very human Edinburgh police detective John Rebus has musical tastes that reflect his age and his personality. Stuck in a case, there are times when only Leonard Cohen will do and on other occasions we are allowed a glimpse of his unkempt flat, the dirty dishes in the sink and the unmade bed to the background sound of The Rolling Stones or Van Morrison.

When I was very young I came across a novel called *A Tree Grows in Brooklyn* by Betty Smith and soon after watched the black and white film on television. Set in the early decades of the 20th century, it is peopled by strong women struggling to survive, but the central male character, the father of the family, is defined by music. He is gentle and charming, witty and imaginative and an alcoholic. He worked as a singing waiter and his beautiful singing voice among the steaming plates of meat and cabbage seemed to be a symbol of a wasted life.

EXERCISE

Write a story where a piece of music turns your main character into a time traveller, going back to a specific moment in the past. As a result they are forced to reflect on their life now and the choices made.

It can be music that has a special resonance for you, something that has been central to your own life. Use your experiences as a resource without turning it into autobiography. That means the character is not you, not a bit like you. Try changing gender. You can write a woman if you are a man, you can take on a male persona if you're a woman.

You're a writer – you can do anything, go anywhere. The only limit is your imagination and the more you exercise it the more it will stretch.

Or write about a time or place that is totally outside your experience. Research it. Plough through Youtube and the music collections of friends. Transport an elderly woman back to the arms of a stranger during World War II because she happens to hear a dash of Glen Miller on the radio; a powerful chief executive becomes an acne-raddled 13 year old again when he hears The Clash's *London Calling* escape from a window cleaner's ipod.

And read *The Dead*. Trust me, you can take good writing without being demolished. You can use the story as a model if you can hear the women's skirts hitting the skirting boards as they waltz around the room. Or you can hate it, be bored by the middle class preoccupations of people who don't interest you. Remember you're a writer and a reader: you can do anything.

The only two things you can't do is
not read
not write.

TERM TWO

HIT AND MISS BIBLIOMANCY

"For a long time now I have tried simply to write the best I can. Sometimes I have good luck and write better than I can"

Ernest Hemingway

If you've ever squirreled away time from a busy life in order to write only to stare at a blank computer screen these two exercises will help.

Technically bibliomancy is making a prediction by opening a book at random, but in our case it involves getting over the fear of starting and having the courage to write even though you don't know where you are going.

EXERCISE I
Pick up a dictionary and choose three words at random.

On my first attempt this particular morning I got:

Waltz – unfortunate – February.

Those three words are almost a story in themselves and for me the setting is the American Civil War – I have no idea why. It probably conjures up something completely different for you. That was a bit too easy so I tried a second time and got something less obvious.

Cave – scum – almanac

Double check the meanings (I consulted The Oxford English Reference Dictionary)

ALMANAC noun. An annual book containing a calendar of months and days and usually other information of a general or specialist nature.

CAVE noun and verb. A large hollow in the side of a cliff or hill or underground. To subside, collapse or give into pressure (cave in). In British public school slang: a warning call or to be a look out (keep cave).

SCUM noun and verb. Layer of dirt, froth or impurities forming at the top of liquid, especially as a result of boiling or fermentation. The most worthless part of something or a worthless person.

There are a couple of ways of tackling this exercise and your method may depend on your mood or the time you have available.

Method One: You have to use the words exactly as they appear. This is best if you have less than half an hour

This could give you an image of a well-thumbed book of useful information, sitting on a country window sill, its pages curling as the weeks and months pass. Perhaps SCUM is frothing in a nearby CAVE pool, a sign of pollution and a symbol that all is not well in the rural idyll...

Method Two: think of the words as themes.

My central character is either an alpha male Caveman-type with authoritarian opinions or a troglodyte (cave dweller) who socially and mentally wants to hide away, happiest living on the margins, observing rather than participating. Perhaps I don't have to choose.

They could be a couple, not a very happy couple, but an interesting one.

Almanac suggests the idea that there is a natural order – is that what Mr and Mrs think or are they working against it? And scum. That could be an insult hurled in rage and I am back to my caveman again. I really don't like him but I am going to enjoy writing him. I see this couple living within an enclosed community – a village, an amateur dramatic society, a bridge club, a political party, Parent Teachers Association, a volunteer group – and...and...and...I'm not sure. It could be that we see their lives through the annual programme of events and something happens. One thing is for sure, they are not the same at the end of the year as they are at the beginning.

EXERCISE II

Emerging writers are often told to write what they know. This is an exercise in writing what you don't know. Go to your computer and find Wikipedia. In the left hand column you can click for a random article. Click it four times – you're allowed to throw one away. Make a story out of the three you have left

This is what I came up with:

- Short biography of an accountant who became Lord Mayor of London in the 1990s
- A small asteroid first discovered in 1989
- List of Gambia's diplomatic missions throughout the world
- A butterfly called the Tiny Flat found in the Kutch region of India

My gut feeling was to ditch the asteroid. So I thought about a male accountant attached to the British embassy in India. He's stuffy and career-driven, but something in him is awoken by India. An amateur naturalist, he falls in love with a member of staff at the Gambian mission. It is inconvenient for all sorts of reasons (both married to other people? I don't know yet, but whatever the problem it has to be serious enough to scupper career plans) and their love lasts as long as the short life span of the Tiny Flat that they come to know on their walks. Only for both of them it is the one true love of their life. In the last scene the man presides at the Lord Mayor's Procession that winds its way through London every year in November. This is the apex of his career and he is resplendent in a fur-edged scarlet gown with lace at his throat and ancient chains of office dangling from his neck. And then, out of the corner of his eye, at the moment when he has it all, when there is nothing more to achieve, he sees a limousine bearing the diplomatic plates of the Gambia. He is taken back to the day he and the woman he loved woke up small dun coloured butterflies from their sleep as they walked hand in hand through the Indian grasslands.

I would have to do some more research but yes, there is a Gambian Mission in New Delhi.

Try it. Go to Wikipedia and choose your three features. Stick with them – make them work.

THE POWER OF THREE...
and other speech writing techniques

"To talk well and eloquently is a very great art, but that an equally great one is to know the right moment to stop"
Wolfgang Amadeus Mozart

A tricolon is a sentence made up of three clearly defined parts. It's a literary device often used in speeches. Here's a few examples:

Veni, vidi, vici (I came; I saw; I conquered.)
Julius Caesar

With malice toward none, with charity toward all, with firmness in the right...
Abraham Lincoln in his second inaugural address.

Education, Education, Education
Tony Blair's priorities in the run up to the 1997 election.

Comedians know how to exploit tricolons. Two is the smallest pattern possible, and the listener or reader will assume that the pattern is going to continue. Confound that expectation by adding a twist and you add humour as in Mark Twain's often quoted observation: There are three kinds of lies: lies, damned lies, and statistics.

President Barack Obama used the power of three 29 times in his victory speech in 2008. Here are two excellent examples. There are many ways he could have expressed these ideas but none would have been so vivid or so memorable.

> ...*(our campaign) began in the backyards of Des Moines and the living rooms of Concord and the front porches of Charleston.*

> ...*(the campaign fund) was built by working men and women who dug into what little savings they had to give $5 and $10 and $20 to the cause.*

He also used other rhetorical techniques such as contrast, repetition and imagery. He could have simply named the towns where the campaign had begun, instead his words allowed us into the homes of his supporters. John Kennedy in his 1960 Inaugural Address used imagery to inspire. '...the energy, the faith, the devotion which we bring to this endeavour will light our country and all who serve it. And the glow from that fire can truly light the world."

I love the repetition that Winston Churchill used in a wartime speech when addressing pupils at his former school: "this is the lesson: never give in, never give in, never, never, never, never – in nothing, great or small, large or petty – never give in except to convictions of honour and good sense." You can hear his voice in those words and also I think the genuine fear of invasion.

So, how can you, as a creative writer, use these techniques? Assuming that you haven't got ambitions to be a speechwriter, you could explore the humorous possibilities. The rule of three could structure a scene, form the basis of a joke, or bring down a pompous character by displaying his inadequacies as well as make a good speaker sound better. You could also integrate the verbal dexterity into prose because there's a beauty and simplicity to these techniques. And a rhythm.

And returning to Obama and Churchill, brilliant speeches can also be a reminder of the compelling intensity that one syllable words can have:

Yes We Can

The news from France is very bad...

EXERCISE

Here's a task that I set a class of 15 students a few years ago. The results were laugh out loud funny.

You've won the Pulitzer or the Booker or the Nobel Prize for Literature. Or an Oscar for a screenplay. Write your acceptance speech.

LISTEN UP – THIS CHAIR IS SPEAKING TO YOU

"We have to continually be jumping off cliffs and developing our wings on the way down"

Kurt Vonnegut

Personification is probably the most common figure of speech and I bet you will come across several examples during the course of the day. It injects human behaviour into material objects or abstract concepts.

Advertisers use it to give a warm voice to the things they want to sell, health educators use it to make vegetables exciting to small children and we use it all the time when we talk and when we write: shoes kill us, colours scream, a furious sea hits the coast.

I've just watched a television advert that talks about cancer as if it were a local bully – Up Yours Cancer! – and another that portrays a garden shed as a demanding baby who will not be soothed by a giant bottle of milk. Only a coat of special wood paint will stop it crying. (No, I didn't get the logic either.)

Our own mortality is so dreadful to contemplate that almost every culture has used personification to describe our feelings about it. There are the Four Horsemen of the Apocalypse in the New Testament (usually named as war, famine, disease and death) and in many countries Death has been depicted as a serious farm worker (the grim reaper) or an old woman with a broom.

In Emily Dickenson's poem he is a gentleman with impeccable good manners.

> *Because I could not stop for Death--*
> *He kindly stopped for me--*
> *The Carriage held but just Ourselves--*
> *And Immortality.*

Personification can pack a punch. You can hear the poet's anger in these lines from *The Mask of Anarchy* by Percy Shelley. It was written in 1819 not long after cavalry charged into an unarmed crowd of men, women and children demanding parliamentary reform in Manchester in the north of England. About 20 died and over 400 were wounded. The tragedy shocked the country and it became known as the Peterloo Massacre (the Battle of Waterloo was four years earlier).

You don't need to know anything about the politicians he mentions to get the message.

> *I met Murder on the way*
> *He had a mask like Castlereagh*
> *Next came Fraud, and he had on,*
> *Like Eldon, an ermined gown;*
> *His big tears, for he wept well,*
> *Turned to mill-stones as they fell.*
> *And the little children, who*
> *Round his feet played to and fro,*
> *Thinking every tear a gem,*
> *Had their brains knocked out by them.*

Personification can bring big things down to a level we can understand and turn the ordinary into something we can look at with new eyes.

This phrase comes from John Steinbeck's short story *Flight* (and is a nice bit of alliteration too).

Five-fingered ferns hung over the water and dropped spray from their fingertips...

SHORT EXERCISE

Change the verbs in CAPITAL LETTERS to a word or phrase that is used to describe very human behaviour.

Add more detail if you want and feel free to change the structure of the sentence. There's no need to stick rigidly to what you see here. For example instead of a petal falling from the rose you could have the rose crying petals. (Sorry, that's really saccharine isn't it?)

Here's a better example where I have extended the personification theme. So, instead of the boy's bedroom door OPENED...

...The boy's bedroom door yawned wide to reveal the mess within. Lethargic football shirts lazed over the back of a chair and a tumble of school books dozed under a scrum of muddy shorts.

Now you have a go:

The kitten MIAOWED when I left for work.

The tree branches SWAYED in the wind.

The cursor MOVES across the computer screen.

LONG EXERCISE

Tony Spiers in *Brighton Ventriloquies*, a poetry pamphlet published by Pighog, gives a voice not only to people who once walked the city streets such as music hall comedian Max Miller and the Prince Regent, but also to less articulate objects that are an essential part of the city: herring gulls, salt and the sea itself.

What kind of vocabulary does ice cream have? What are its secret icy thoughts and what does it think of us?

LISTEN UP – THIS CHAIR IS SPEAKING TO YOU

spare us their scold
for we are unvisited snow
brides of the light

unlicked vanillas, keep us cool
who knows what been in
those stanching gapes, whorehouses

Look around. The sturdy dark brown bookcase in the corner: is it male or female? Cheerful or depressed? Could the corkscrew on the desk be on a diet? Is the bargain basement table a bit sneaky? An antique leather armchair and an Ikea kitchen stool may do similar jobs, but they would have very different ways of looking at the world.

In poetry or prose personify a piece of furniture you know well. Perhaps it has been in the family since you were born. Perhaps you bought it last week. Give it a name if you want, but you must give it an attitude.

THOU SHALL NOT

"Don't say it was delightful; make us say delightful when we've read the description. You see, all those words (horrifying, wonderful, hideous, exquisite) are only like saying to your readers, please will you do the job for me"
C.S.Lewis

The focus in this section is on creating a convincing sense of place, but I also want you to do something else at the same time. I want you to generate a forbidding atmosphere, the sense that the character you are writing about shouldn't be there.

That could be because the place itself is dangerous, illicit, secret. Or the place could be quite ordinary – a garden shed, a playground, someone's room – but your character is breaking the rules by being there.

You can write in the first person (I said, I hid in the shadows) or the third person (he whispered, she tiptoed) whatever feels comfortable.

As this exercise is about rule breaking and childhood is hedged in by rules you may find that your instinct is to write from your own experience.

That's fine, and worth doing even if your goal is to be a best-selling thriller writer. Remember that these exercises are practice, designed to support your real writing. Here your aim is to create an edgy look-behind-you atmosphere and an environment that the reader can believe in – all perfect ingredients for an action novel.

Choose the place. Visualise it. Walk around it in your imagination.

I'm a great believer in thinking with a pen in your hand, so make some notes for yourself. No one will ever see them. They only exist so you can start translating the pictures in your head into words.

It often helps to go through the five senses again – a single word will do, but if a phrase leaps out then grab it and write it down. Don't worry about whether it is a cliché at this stage. This is all about gathering information. You can put it into your own words, using the kind of language you want to write, later.

Name three sounds you could HEAR If you were standing in this place and you shut your eyes.

Name three odours you could SMELL if you were standing in this place and you shut your eyes.

Still with your eyes shut, imagine that you are kneeling down. What can you feel beneath you? If you were to stretch out a hand what would you TOUCH? Are you warm or cold? If you are inside is there a draught? If you are outside is there a wind?

Your mouth is dry. You lick your lips. What can you TASTE? What else?

Stand up: open your eyes. Three words to describe what you can SEE straight in front of you. Look up: what's above your head?

You won't use all this information, you may only use a few words, but it will be easier to compose a compelling description if you know what it is like to be there.

It is tempting to rely on adjectives to give an impression of mood but they can clog up sentences. Verbs are full of energy and the right verb can do the work of a complicated adjective-choked phrase in half the space and without giving the reader indigestion.

In *Wuthering Heights* Emily Brontë describes chairs lurking in the shade and dogs haunting the shadowy corners of the house. In Will Self's collection of short stories *Liver: a Fictional Organ,* a character makes tea. Tea bags are slung into cups and hot death rains down.

You can do the same thing in your own writing. For example if you were describing a grim urban scene you might want to say something like:

The wind blew rubbish across the street

You could lower the temperature by ditching the verb blew for something sharper.

The wind knifed across the street driving the rubbish before it

You might want to add some visual detail.

The wind knifed across the street driving the sweet wrappers and takeaway containers into the gutters

But maybe that is too much emphasis on what the street looks like and you want the reader to feel what it is like to be in the street.

The wind knifed across the street stinging eyes and burning cheeks as it drove eddies of rubbish before it.

Is that too much information?

None of these sentences are wrong. You have to ask yourself if they express what you want to say in the way you want to say it. You may in the end decide to pare back and forget all about the rubbish.

The wind knifed across the street

With all the information you've gathered about the place you are a ready to make a reader feel the way you want them to feel. You're in control. This exercise is in two parts.

EXERCISE I

Describe the scene you've chosen, concentrating on the atmosphere.

How much you write depends on you, but I suggest a maximum of 300 words or two pages of handwriting (always supposing you don't write in large capitals – in which case give yourself three pages.)

EXERCISE II

Cut by at least 20%. Don't cheat (or if you do, remember you're only cheating yourself).

Adjectives do not get lonely: they don't have to travel in pairs. Limit yourself to one adjective per sentence. Or do without completely. Examine every verb. If walked can be transformed into stumble or crept it might be possible to cut a few more words. Cut out whole sentences even if they are elegant and beautifully crafted (especially if they are elegant and beautifully crafted). If they don't add to the uneasy atmosphere, they have to go. .

You are not allowed ANY adverbs, not one. For some writers this will make cutting the first draft easy peasy. Yes, adverbs have a place in the English language, but not here and not today. This is an experiment in discovering what life is like without them.

To be clear, adverbs adjust or modify an adjective by adding information. Although they frequently end in -ly, that is not a guarantee that a word is an adverb. For example, the words *lovely and lonely* are respectable adjectives and should be left alone. However, in the phrase quite lonely – quite is an adverb. Cut them all. We use them to add emphasis, but often they have the opposite effect. Stephen King believes they are a sign of the timid writer who is scared that the reader won't be convinced by what's on the page, so sleeves are tugged as the writer whispers: yes, honestly, as bad as that...

Still not persuaded? Let's look at an ordinary, everyday sentence:-

He grabbed the steering wheel firmly.

Nothing wrong with that you might say, but how do you grab something softy, weakly? The verb has already done the work.

He grabbed the steering wheel.

There's a direct simplicity in the adverb-less sentences plus a sense of urgency because it's shorter.

Be brave and see what it feels like without adverbs and without padding. This is an experiment – if you're not strict with yourself then you can't judge the effect when you cut every word you can do without. Look out for any other useless words. I'm a devil for *just*. I had to cut it out of the sentence above.

Reduce your original 300 words to 240 (or less)
Reduce 80 words to around 64

Compare the two versions. What have you cut from the first version that is essential? Put it back. Maybe the editing exercise has given you the chance to think about new material that will improve the original. Add it. But you cannot go over the word count of your first draft whether it was 300 words or just 80.

THE FOUR LINE POEM

"Poetry began when somebody walked off of a savanna or out of a cave and looked up at the sky with wonder and said, 'Ahhh'. That was the first poem"

Lucille Clifton

Poetry is concentrated. A poet can pack more into a few lines than most of us can cover in a couple of pages of prose.

It can tackle the big subjects: love and loss, passion and heartache. The trouble is these are all abstract concepts. Love is an idea that exists in your head and in my head, but how do we know that when you talk about love or hate or fear that it means the same thing to both of us? The short answer is you don't, especially as each emotion has so many qualities. The fear of losing your lover is very different to the fear of hearing footsteps behind you in a dark alley.

One way a poet can overcome this problem is by creating a picture in the reader's mind of something concrete, something that is visible and touchable, something which we both understand. Well-crafted imagery isn't only beautiful, it is also an effective means of communication.

EXERCISE

I got this exercise many years ago from the poet and novelist Naomi Foyle. She has a doctorate in poetry so you know it's good. Naomi's written a cyber-thriller set in South Korea, been a poetry editor and published several poetry collections including a ballad about Grace O' Malley, the pirate queen of Tudor Ireland. I had the privilege of appearing in the stage version so I know what an accomplished poet she is.

Below is a list of emotions. I'm not going to ask you to shut your eyes and pick one. This time you get to choose which one you want to work on. You could come back and work your way through the entire list if you want.

- Anger
- Love
- Confusion
- Grief
- Irritation
- Depression
- Happiness
- Contentment

Your job is to give the reader a clear understanding of the emotion you are writing about because the pictures you create are so precise that there's no mistaking what you mean. I don't want you to mention the emotion in the poem at all or a word close to it. So, for example, if your subject is depression you can't have sadness or melancholy or any other abstract synonym.

Although this is intended to be a short poem, just four lines long, these are rubber rules. Expand it if you want, but never waver from the concept of describing abstract concepts through concrete images.

Line One

The first line describes the emotion as a colour. Choose one that reflects the intensity of the emotion. Be specific. Not just any old brown but as brown as a bruise or a ploughed field in March. As pink as a strawberry milk shake or a mouth ulcer....

Make it personal. This is your poem. It could be as pink as the faded gingham aprons in Miss Mott's cookery class.

THE FOUR LINE POEM

Hit the reader between the eyes. That means no clichés and not settling for the first idea that comes to mind. Work at it. No one ever said being fresh and original was going to be easy.

And please, please avoid wordy waffle. You're not allowed anything that resembles:-

> *...the unimaginable darkness where the culmination of eternal galaxies swirl in an indescribable ballet of cascading sovereignty...*

In fact, never use the words indescribable and unimaginable in any context. You're a writer – your job is to describe and imagine. You may fail, but you have to try.

Line Two
The second line starts with the words: It feels like...
Be wary – it is easy to slip into the abstract with a phrase such as it feels like perfect peace. Remember, it has to be something a reader can physically experience. Go for something along the lines of: stroking velvet or grabbing barbed wire (only better, of course).

Line Three:
The third line begins with: It sounds like...
The example I have is a dog tied up in a garden, but you might want to develop the image. As readers we love detail. It allows us to go beyond the words, and enter the story, but it has to be the right detail – we need pictures more than we need information. If you're writing about a dog I don't want to know about Kennel Club breeds, but I do want bark-coloured teeth; hot, meaty breath and a velvet muzzle.

Line Four:
The fourth line begins: It happens when...
When the alarm clock goes off perhaps, or when the children run out from school...when you see the date on the calendar or when she or he walks into the room (which, depending on the emotion is either a head-on-one-side ah! Or a goosebump ohhh)...Go for it. You'll find something special.

Now you have a poem AND you've made an extraordinary effort to get a reader to feel what you feel, to share your thoughts. If it has worked the reader will also be able to hear your voice even if you never meet.

WRITING FUNNY EVEN THOUGH YOU CAN'T TELL A JOKE

"Laughter is wine for the soul – laughter soft, or loud and deep, tinged through with seriousness – the hilarious declaration made by man that life is worth living"
Seán O'Casey

No one laughs when you deliver a joke, so how can you do funny?

Telling a joke is a live performance that requires a wide range of specific skills from an excellent memory to getting the pauses between the words just right. Writing funny is exactly the same except you inject comedy timing by the way you structure your writing and pressing enter is so much easier than facing an audience.

I'm not pretending it is easy though. There's a special magic in being able to make someone laugh, but it is a magic that can be sharpened by practice.

You might wonder why you should tiptoe onto this territory when serious subjects attract you. You want to write about the passions that tear people apart and the important issues that rock worlds. You don't do funny.

I think there are two main reasons why any writer should consider playing around with humour.

First, it's a question of light and dark. The dark will seem darker if there are moments of lightness. Think about Shakespeare's *Macbeth*. Just after all the drama and violence of Duncan's murder there's a knocking on the castle gates. The dreadful rhythm is insistent. Whoever is outside wants to come in and when they do they will discover that the King has been murdered. The atmosphere was already taut and now the tension heightens which each knock.

What happens? Is the body discovered? Is Macbeth denounced as a traitor? Does he talk his way out of it or fight his way out?

No, instead a drunk porter staggers to the door and tells the impatient noblemen that alcohol is responsible for nose-picking, sleep and urine. He goes on to explain that it is a popular fallacy to think that alcohol aids love making. "...it provokes the desire but takes away the performance...it sets him on and it takes him off; it persuades him and disheartens him; it makes him stand to and not stand to..."

It's low, basic humour about body functions and a wonderful scene for a clown with a gift for physical comedy and there was always at least one in Shakespeare's troupe of actors. It breaks the tension, but it doesn't destroy it. The body is still waiting to be discovered, but we can breathe again. The comic interval allows the audience to sit back and wait for the rest of the story to open out. Keep the tension at the same pitch and it would be like a soprano trilling out an aria on the same top note, going on and on and on and on.

The second reason I think it's worth exploring the techniques of comedy is that I'm convinced that all these separate literary categories feed and support each other.

Want to be a novelist? It does no harm to go on a screenwriting course where the plot will be discussed before the first word is written. In love with flash fiction? Read a poet who knows the power of a few words. Comedy is all about confounding expectations – an excellent tool for any storyteller.

Ok, those are the arguments why you should give humour a chance. In this exercise we are going to look at a straightforward parody, but first a few definitions because these words get thrown about and it's not always clear what is meant by them.

PARODY – imitating the work of another in a way that's obvious to the reader or viewer. It can mock, using humour as a weapon, or be a gentle swipe, revealing the ridiculous in something we take for granted. Or you can parody a structure – such as a shopping list – because of the contrast with the subject you're writing about: the shopping list of a suicide bomber, for example. The essential element is that the reader has to be familiar with what's being parodied.

PASTICHE – the word can be used to describe a jumble of styles but is more often used for another kind of imitation. Again, there's no attempt to hide the fact from the reader/viewer, but here the motive is always benign – you don't create a pastiche of something you dislike. It's a compliment even when it's funny and it should work in its own right as a passage of writing even when the reader doesn't know the original.

Quentin Tarantino's film *Kill Bill* is a pastiche – in both senses of the word – to Hong Kong martial arts films, Japanese sword-fighting films and spaghetti westerns. (By the way, *Kill Buljo* is a 2007 Norwegian parody of *Kill Bill*.)

PLAGIARISM – is theft. It's copying someone else's work and passing it off as your own. If you can do it, you don't steal it. And if you can't do it, you will be found out sooner rather than later.

The roots of all three words reveal the true meaning: parody comes to us from the Greek for a comic song, pastiche is a French word that evolved out of the Italian pasticcio meaning a pie, or something blended together, and plagiare is Latin for kidnap or abduct which is still a pretty good working definition of plagiarism.

EXERCISE
In this exercise you are asked to parody entries in a dictionary. So far so good, because even if you haven't consulted one in ages, you

know how it works and you also know the kind of language employed and your reader will too. However, better than that, I can offer you a wonderful example that you can use as a model. Remember there are only two ways to learn how to write: write as much as you can and read as much as you can – *The Devil's Dictionary* is one of the things you should read.

Published over a hundred years ago, it hasn't been out of print since. The author was Ambrose Bierce, an American journalist and author. His dictionary entries first appeared in a San Francisco newspaper in the 1880s and he used his sharp wit to deflate the pompous and highlight social problems that concerned him. The end of his life is a mystery though. He was thought to be reporting on the Mexican Rebellion and the last letter he wrote was dated December 26th 1913. He wasn't heard of again.

Here's a small sample from his dictionary.

AIR A nutritious substance supplied by a bountiful Providence for the fattening of the poor.
BACKBITE To speak of a man as you find him when he can't find you.
BORE A person who talks when you wish him to listen.
BRUTE See *HUSBAND*.
CLAIRVOYANT A person, commonly a woman, who has the power of seeing that which is invisible to her patron, namely, that he is a blockhead.
COWARD One who in a perilous emergency thinks with his legs.
DAWN The time when men of reason go to bed. Certain old men prefer to rise at about that time, taking a cold bath and a long walk with an empty stomach, and otherwise mortifying the flesh. They then point with pride to these practices as the cause of their sturdy health and ripe years; the truth being that they are hearty and old, not because of their habits, but in spite of them. The reason we find only robust persons doing this thing is that it has killed all the others who have tried it.
DICTIONARY A malevolent literary device for cramping the growth of a language and making it hard and inelastic. This dictionary, however, is a most useful work.
DIPLOMACY The patriotic art of lying for one's country.

FIDELITY A virtue peculiar to those who are about to be betrayed.
GENEROUS Originally this word meant noble by birth and was rightly applied to a great multitude of persons. It now means noble by nature and is taking a bit of a rest.

It's a gem, isn't it? Some of it is dated, but much of it is still laugh out loud funny. You can download the complete dictionary for free from Project Gutenberg at http://www.gutenberg.org/ebooks/972

Make your own Devil's Dictionary. What would Ambrose have made of:

- The Internet
- Ebay
- Ebooks
- Blogs

You might feel that words like fashion, music and banking also need to be re-defined.

Or perhaps a more specialised dictionary is needed. A mother's dictionary might re-define such words as washing machine and sleep: a shop assistant's dictionary might shed new light on the true meaning of one-size-fits-all while a writer's dictionary might take a sharper look at reviewers, deadlines and word counts...

BE AFRAID.
BE VERY AFRAID

"At night, when the objective world has slunk back into its cavern and left dreamers to their own, there come inspirations and capabilities impossible at any less magical and quiet hour. No one knows whether or not he is a writer unless he has tried writing at night"

H.P. Lovecraft

Lovecraft was born into the age of gaslight and candles, but writing with a flavour of the night is still popular. It comes in many varieties. Horror subgenres range from the psychological to the gothic, from vampire to cyber punk (think gritty low life in a futuristic high tech society) and then there is Lovecraftian literature where feeble man acts in an incomprehensible universe. First, last and always, horror fiction is about making the reader afraid.

A horror story needs three essential ingredients – suspense, atmosphere and the right subject.

In this exercise I'm going to deal with SUSPENSE. Too many films and books are steeped in the horrible at the expense of the sensation that lifts the hairs on the back of the neck. Gore might give bad dreams, but suspense properly handled makes you leap out of your cinema seat or persuades you that someone is reading over your shoulder.

To see how it works I will take a well-worn horror story line – the kind we have seen or read a score of times. The fear at the heart of this story is perhaps the most basic fear of all; fear of being killed or maimed. Here it is coupled with the fear of being hunted. This fear kept our cavemen and women ancestors alive and is hardwired into us, crossing boundaries and cultures.

I've broken this basic horror story into FOUR key elements.

ONE
The reader knows what to be afraid of.
In a classic horror story the central character might hear a news report of an axe murderer escaping from prison, for example. The danger is upfront, clear and apparent.

TWO
Expectations are created by identifying the nature of the threat.
Perhaps the house where the main character lives is near the prison. Or it could be that the home-alone central character is a prison guard and revenge could be a motive for an attack.

THREE
A series of small mini climaxes heighten tension and offer a moment of relief. The scratching at the window isn't the axe man trying to break in, but the branches of a tree knocking against the glass; the shadowy figure in the porch turns out to be the vicar rattling a collecting tin.

FOUR
Expectations are realised. The final tap-tap-tapping at the front door is the axe man with a smile across his face and the vicar's severed head in his hand.

Converted into four steps this seems very trite and formulaic, especially with the examples I've chosen, but if you add characters with whom the reader could identify it is the stuff of nightmares. Replace the axe murderer with a student stalking a wheelchair-using university lecturer or an obsessive former lover incensed by the birth of a baby...This is the kind of story you could read in a newspaper – this is the kind of story that has the power to haunt readers.

When thinking about how to inject suspense into your story you could do worse than watch the first *Alien* film again. Spoiler alert. Skip the rest of this if you've never seen it. Stop writing, stop reading and go and find a copy to watch right now. This counts as essential research.

For the rest of us, remember when Ripley – Sigourney Weaver's character – the last surviving crew member, is about to blow up the space ship and escape in a pod? When we watched it for the very first time we might have glanced at the clock at that point and realised that the film was going to end soon. We sat there secure in the knowledge that her plan was going to work and all would be well.

And then she decides to go back for Jonesy the cat...

At that point even ardent cat lover's must have been screaming: No! Save yourself!

In a beautifully executed final mini climax, she does rescue puss and blow up the ship. Together they head back to the safety of Earth... only not on their own.

The best way of thinking about how techniques like this can be applied to your own writing is with a pen in your hand. For that reason, I've devised a suspense template that I often use in writing classes.

I've done the opening lines for you. Notice that although it dives straight in without any explanation, it does suggest danger is very near.

SUSPENSE EXERCISE TEMPLATE
STEP ONE
She hurried down the path. She had to get away.

STEP TWO
Describe who 'they' are.

STEP THREE
They are getting closer

STEP FOUR
Closer still

STEP FIVE
She hides – they miss her

STEP SIX
It seems safe

STEP SEVEN
It isn't. She is nearly caught.

STEP EIGHT
She runs again

STEP NINE
Safe. (Or not – you choose.)

By the way, you could adapt the template to fit a sports story, a war drama or a crime action scene. It works for any situation where the outcome is uncertain.

SIZE MATTERS

"I learned that you should feel when writing, not like Lord Byron on a mountain top, but like a child stringing beads in kindergarten – happy, absorbed and quietly putting one bead on after another"

Brenda Ueland

I love this exercise. It is so simple and so effective. All you have to do is write a very long sentence and then a collection of short sentences.

Why?

Because the different textures can control the atmosphere of a scene in much the same way as an actor can portray impatience by pacing across the stage, picking up a newspaper and putting it down again. He is eloquent without a word of dialogue.

Consider the difference between:

She died last Tuesday morning in the County Hospital after a long illness.

And

She's dead.

Short can also suggest speed. Flick through any popular thriller and you will find that the opening chapters introducing the characters and the challenges they face are of a conventional length. Then something dramatic happens, perhaps a car chase. The sentences get shorter. The words get shorter. The chapters are short. As readers we may not notice, all we'll know is that this is an action packed novel.

So, what can long sentences do?

They can express boredom, opulence or – as in this sentence from Charles Dickens's *Oliver Twist* – produce a galloping meld of vivid word pictures

> *We behold, with throbbing bosoms, the heroine in the grasp of a proud and ruthless baron: her virtue and her life alike in danger, drawing forth her dagger to preserve the one at the cost of the other; and just as our expectations are wrought up to the highest pitch, a whistle is heard, and we are straightway transported to the great hall of the castle; where a grey-headed seneschal sings a funny chorus with a funnier body of vassals, who are free of all sorts of places, from church vaults to palaces, and roam about in company, carolling perpetually.*

(100 words)

Piling impression upon impression to build a multi-layered picture isn't confined to Victorian novels. Here's a description of an aerobics class....

> *Marble arms slicing through water, the sound of the instructor's CD player ricocheting off the swimming pool walls, ten bodies arching, splashing, kicking in an unsteady formation to the echoes of a forgotten boy band, and afterwards we peel off our second-skin swimming costumes and feel as virtuous as if we'd been to church or watched a re-run of* The Waltons.

(A paltry 60 words)

EXERCISE

Describe a room in just one sentence. It can be real or imaginary, the important thing is to use as many words as you can, perhaps piling clause upon clause or by making a list. Count the words when you're finished and see how many you can fit in while still making sense and obeying the usual rules of English.

Here's an example of what I have in mind, but you can probably do much longer.

> *The dust-encrusted gilt on the antique picture frames and the ancient velvet curtains, purchased before fascism was born, were set on fire by the early morning light shining through the stained glass window and brought the collection of oil paintings to new, vibrant life while transforming the swathes of muslin draping the four poster bed into an opal waterfall of translucent shadows.*

(62 words)

Now describe the same room using sentences that are no longer than six words. Don't moan – there's a reason for setting such a mean limit. Six words forces you to think about every picture you're attempting to create and every word in your armoury.

Oh, and don't forget this is prose. No fancy impressionistic, poetic stanzas which just happen to have very few words. You can't get away with writing in note form either. I want proper sentences with capital letters and full stops, with conjunctions (and, but, so etc) and indefinite articles (the, a, an) – I think they are called determiners in American English – subjects, objects and all the rest of the grammar shebang.

Here's my example:

> *The light shone through stained glass. The oil paintings were alive. Dawn set the picture frames alight. Ancient gilt turned into gold. Muslin turned into water.*

I quite like this, especially the last line, but it is only an exercise. If this were part of a story or a novel I would want to add more textual variety. Something like:

> *The oil paintings leapt into life. The early morning light shone through the bedroom' s stained glass window and set the picture frames alight. Dusty gilt became gold. Muslin turned into water.*

Using sentences of different lengths adds interest. As readers we like variety and sentences trotted out with the same construction, time after time, soon beat a tum-te-tum tune in our head and that can become tum-te... isn't there something on television?

A writer must never forget just how easy it is to put a book down. It's easier than switching channels with a remote. It's easier than texting a friend.

You can shatter rules, fool around with ideas and conventions, break new ground, confuse, perplex, lie to the reader even, but what you can't do is bore them. Because a bored reader very soon stops being a reader.

Experiment with this exercise and apply it to a page of your 'real' writing. We all favour certain words and therefore over use them and the same is often true with sentences, the building bricks of prose. I'm not suggesting you should change your style of writing, but I do think it is important you are aware of it and that you make conscious decisions rather than stick to a comfortable groove.

MMMM, FEEL THE COFFEE, TASTE THE TEAPOT

"Memory should not be thought of as a noun – a storehouse or recording machine – but as a verb; an activity that makes patterns out of consciousness"

Suzanne Langer

Your subject is breakfast this morning. And you can't get away with saying you didn't have breakfast because, unless you are starving, in which case put this book down and go find something to eat, you broke your fast at some point during the day.

However, before we get down to the actual exercise I want to acknowledge how hard it is to describe flavour and mention some strategies we can employ to meet the challenge. I've already mentioned that English doesn't have an extensive vocabulary for the way something tastes, as a glance at any magazine wine column will reveal. Here is an example:

oak and throaty cherries
smells of thyme, bay and dry olive groves

Taken out of context, I have no idea whether these descriptions mean the wine in question was good or bad, one to drink or one to avoid, but I understand the problem the writer has.

Imagine describing what an orange is like to someone who has never eaten one. Comparisons help. It's like a lemon, but bigger, sweeter, rounder and it's a different colour, richer, with a dash of red in the yellow, more than a dash... The problem is harder if your reader doesn't know what a lemon is either.

Nigel Slater is a chef who writes about food. He is very aware of flavour and also has a good memory for the food of his childhood. In his memoir *Toast* he recalls the magical qualities of butterscotch Angel Delight which managed to taste of both sugar and soap at the same time. He also notes that cream soda was like drinking a sponge cake.

Sometimes to get close to the experience of eating texture becomes more important than taste. This description is from Deidre Madden's novel *Remembering Light and Stone*:

> *I pulled the cornetto apart. It was still warm and flaky because it was so fresh. It oozed apricot jam.*

And food isn't always pleasant as John Lancaster describes in *The Debt to Pleasure*

> *... unabashed gristle floated in a mud-coloured sauce whose texture and temperature was powerfully reminiscent of mucus.*

I have a brief warm-up exercise you might like to try. Although it's not directly related to food writing, I think it could help.

First, though, a question: what colour is the letter A? Does a chair grating on the floor taste like burnt toast? Is the opening movement of Beethoven's Eroica a clash of burgundy and blue?

If you don't know what I'm on about you are in good company. Only 3% of the population have a condition called synaesthesia and live in a world of extra sensations. Seeing letters and words in colour is the most common form, followed by experiencing music as both colour and sound. Taste can also play a part and a Russian scientist once interviewed a woman who described a noise as 'something like fireworks tinged with pink-red. The strip of colour feels rough and unpleasant and it has an ugly taste — rather like that of a briny pickle.' That's colour, touch, and taste while the rest of us can only hear.

Famous creative people with synaesthesia include the painter David Hockney, the French composer Olivier Messiaen and the writer Vladimir Nabokov.

Even if we aren't part of the 3% who experience a kind of magical mixing of senses we can use it in our writing. Here's how other writers have done it.

> *With blue, uncertain, stumbling buzz,*
> *Between the light and me;*
> *And then the windows failed, and then*
> *I could not see to see.*

From *I heard a fly buzz when I died* by Emily Dickinson

> *(I do not know what it is about you that closes*
> *and opens; only something in me understands*
> *the voice of your eyes is deeper than all roses)*
> *nobody, not even the rain, has such small hands*

From *somewhere i have never travelled* by e e cummings

> *The lights grow brighter as the earth lurches away from the sun*
> *and now the orchestra is playing yellow cocktail music and the*
> *opera of voices pitches a key higher.*

From *The Great Gatsby* by F. Scott Fitzgerald,

And the cheesiest example of all:

> *On you, wet is my favorite color.*

A line spoken by Elvis in the film *Blue Hawaii* (which is itself an example).

MMMM, FEEL THE COFFEE, TASTE THE TEAPOT

For this very quick exercise, take a sheet of paper and fold it twice lengthways to make three equal columns.

In the first column write a list of ten flavours (sweet, salty, peppery etc); in the middle column write down ten colours and in the last column jot down ten sounds (scream, whisper etc). Now see what you've got by making connections across the page. It's not unusual to talk about a golden voice, have you got a yellow roar? What about a tangy aria or a syrupy pink simper?

If you get one usable descriptive phrase you're doing well, but I hope the exercise has opened up to the possibility of linking different sensations.

Now, finally, the **EXERCISE**

Remember, the subject is today's breakfast.

Describe it and contrast it with other breakfasts you've known: childhood breakfasts, breakfasts with lovers, breakfasts with children, breakfasts in greasy spoon cafes, in chic coffee houses, hung over breakfasts, breakfasts that start with a shot of alcohol, sleep-raddled breakfasts, breakfast when you wake up and know you could rule the world, breakfasts in hospitals, hostels, hotels, in the homes of friends, breakfasts when you have all the time in the world, breakfasts on the run, breakfasts that are really nothing more than a swill of mouthwash and a smear of toothpaste...

The aim of this passage of writing is to make the reader feel as though he or she was there, sitting at the table, smelling the coffee, and, by comparing and contrasting breakfasts that you have known you're writing about life now and life back in a time that you can't re-visit in any other way.

How long?

Aim for 500 words and give yourself permission to write more as memories unfurl...

IT'S THE WAY
THEY SAY IT

"A man once asked me... how I managed in my books to write such natural conversation between men when they were by themselves...I replied that I had coped with this difficult problem by making my men talk, as far as possible, like ordinary human beings"

Dorothy L. Sayers

A word out of place in dialogue shows up as clearly as felt pen squiggles on a wedding dress. There's no book that can tell you how to get it right but you can train your ear. There's a problem if all your characters sound the same – because people don't. There's an even bigger problem if they all sound like you.

Listen to the conversations around you: not just what it is said but also how it is said. Listen to talk shows on radio and television. Tune in to a phone-in and jot down the expressions used by people with opposing views. You probably won't get it word for word, but try to capture the energy and the sense that very different people are talking.

When revising a passage of dialogue use the following questions as a guide.

1) Does the vocabulary fit the age, education and experience of the character who is speaking?

No one – with the possible exception of Stephen Fry – talks in the way they would write. We are much more casual when we speak: can't rather than cannot; don't instead of do not. People usually only speak formally when they want to create an impression – a parent telling a child off, for example, or a person seeking to display their authority.

2) Is the dialogue saying too much?

Characters should never sound as though they are speaking for the benefit of the reader. We are eavesdroppers, not an audience. Dialogue often reveals but it should never *tell*.

An example of how not to do it....

> *"Hello Nick, my best mate since the day we started school. How's your wife Rosie? Remember when she was engaged to me before you two got married."*
> *"Nice to see you Simon. We're fine, apart from Rosie's leg. She's never been the same since the accident. We heard you've been away on some exotic holiday."*
> *"Yes, 14 day African safari. Saw a couple of lions and more elephants than you could count. My new girlfriend loved it but, of course she's a model and used to these kind of trips."*

3) Is it too natural?

Dialogue should come across as real people talking, but without all the ums and ahs that pepper real speech. Cut out the padding and references to the weather and how many sugars a character has in her coffee. Depending on the context you may want to cut out the coffee altogether.

People in books are a good deal more articulate than they would be in real life (pay attention and notice how many times in a day someone doesn't finish a sentence. My children tell me that I rarely reach a full stop.) They also ramble less.

However, just as in real life what they say isn't necessarily what they mean. Subtext, the meaning underneath the words, is what good dialogue is all about.

Would you like another coffee? Could mean anything from *please don't go* to *Get out of here!*

4) Is there anything better than he said she said?

At school we were encouraged to use dialogue tags like gasped, grumbled and groaned instead of said. American bestseller Elmore Leonard, who died while this book was being prepared, maintained that now our teachers have done their job and encouraged us to develop a wide vocabulary we should return to our old ways and only use he said or she said to identify who is speaking.

The great thing about the word said is that the reader is so used to seeing it on the page that they skim over it, only registering who is saying yes and who is saying no. The fluidity – the quality that makes a story as easy to read as a Crème Brûlée is to eat – isn't disrupted.

It seems to me that there are only two exceptions to Elmore Leonard's rule. The first is when the reader couldn't be expected to pick up the way a statement is made in any other way. This often applies to sound: he whispered; she murmured.

The second exception is when it is plain silly, as in the sentence:

'Help! I'm on fire,' she said running out of the room.

I suspect she screamed or yelled. Maybe she even shrieked.

EXERCISE I
First, a warm up:
Create THREE different characters just by the way they respond to this classic question.

"Could you lend me 10 pounds/euros/dollars?"

They are all saying the same thing: NO and they are all saying it in a couple of sentences or less.

How each character phrases their response will reveal something about them and their relationship with the person asking for money. Experiment, but don't make this an information dump.

EXERCISE II
Now for something a bit meatier: write a conversation between two of these characters.

- Spoilt teenager
- Forgetful elderly person
- Someone obsessed with fantasy computer games
- A woman about to lose her job
- A man about to get married

They are discussing something ordinary and unimportant, perhaps a programme they are watching together on television, BUT one suspects the other of underhand behaviour in some way. This is what is felt *beneath* the surface. Reveal their real feelings through the conversation but don't spell it out. At the same time some of their back story may emerge (what's happened in their lives before this scene).

Drip feed information – don't deliver it in chunks. It may help to re-read the conversation between Nick and Simon. They not only reveal too much in an avalanche of back story, Simon also asks an odd question: 'How is your wife Rosie?' Nick knows that his wife is called Rosie so he doesn't need to be reminded of it. The only people who could possibly want to know are readers and dialogue should never sound as though it is written for readers.

Here's a complete re-write of that scene between Nick and Simon.

> *"You're back then. Africa, was it?"*
> *Simon nodded and looked past his old friend at the cars queuing at the traffic lights*

"Lions and gorillas, stuff like that? You'd need a fancy camera for that kind of trip." Nick's voice rose. He leant forward. "No point going otherwise. I'd take a nice bit of equipment on a jaunt like that, I would."

"We took a lot of pictures, yes." Simon glanced at his watch. The lights had changed and the noise of the traffic made it harder to hear.

"You said we. New girlfriend?"

"Not exactly new. We've known each other ages. You must meet her. You and Rosie could come over."

"Rosie doesn't go out much."

"The leg?"

"The leg."

"I think about the driver of that car," Simon said. "He deserved prison for what he did."

"Yeah, we all said that. It doesn't help though. What happened happened. And Rosie and me..." Nick shrugged and the sentence trailed off.

"I do think about her, about both of you. Perhaps I could pop around sometime?"

"What is she, your new girl? Actress? Model? She is, isn't she? I can see it in your face. She's a bloody model. I'll tell Rosie that. What is she topless? Fashion? Rosie will want to know."

"Fashion."

"Of course. Classy." Nick turned away.

Simon called after him. "Tell Rosie, I'll call around. Tell her that." He said it again, louder, even though Nick was too far away to hear.

I didn't include all the information because it was just too much for one conversation, what I added was emotion. In the first how-not-to example the two men were swapping parcels of information for no apparent reason. Now we are starting to see the connections and some of the emotional sub-text is revealed. The fact, for example, that Nick didn't know anything about his friend's girlfriend suggests that the two men no longer move in the same social circles.

You may have noticed that I only used one said. Instead I used actions to identify who was speaking: Nick shrugging, Simon gazing at the traffic.

I did manage to include all three names in this passage, but I think I was pushing at the limit of the reader's patience. Be very careful about how many names you reveal at one time. They are hard to remember in real life and they are hard to remember in a text. Often it is the least interesting thing about a character and as long as there is no danger of a reader being confused about who is speaking, it is something that can often wait until later. In this instance we don't discover the name of Simon's girlfriend. Depending on how the story pans out we may never need to know it.

When you write the dialogue between your own odd couple don't be scared of one word responses. Sometimes they reveal more than a long speech.

TERM THREE

FINDING CHARACTERS IN UNLIKELY PLACES

"Characters take on life sometimes by luck, but I suspect it is when you can write more entirely out of yourself, inside the skin, heart, mind, and soul of a person who is not yourself, that a character becomes in his own right another human being on the page"

Eudora Welty

Before you start this exercise you will need to do some research about an animal, any animal, and find out about its social habits and traits.

Be adventurous in your choice. You CAN have a cat or a dog, but don't choose your own pet because you will end up writing about them and that's not the point. But please don't spend all your precious writing time on research. You don't need to become an expert. For instance, all you need to know about a polar bear is that it's a good parent with great physical strength and a filthy temper.

EXERCISE

You are going to make your animal human and write a character study that will not only give a physical description, but also include an event that reveals their personality.

It may make sense to limit yourself to using just three characteristics. I can see the polar bear as a gangster, a controlling mother or a neighbour from hell. He or she doesn't have to eat walrus as well.

Here's my example:

> *With an office grey complexion, and prominent ears and long nose, the manager was an unimpressive man, although when he leant across the desk to make a point it was clear that the heavy flesh was dense rather than flabby and there was strength in the hands that typed terse emails.*

> *Regularly developing new filing systems and reorganising holiday rotas, his current obsession was the reception area. The new look demanded chocolate leather sofas and faux antique mirrors, but he couldn't make up his mind between taupe walls or duck egg blue.*

> *On Thursday afternoon he announced that he needed an interior design consultant and instructed a member of staff to research a short list. On Friday morning Central Office announced 20 % cuts. There goes the sofas the staff thought, there goes the mirrors with their fake brown blotches and distressed gold frames. They were wrong. By mid morning five administrative assistants were told to clear their desks. The manager was still flicking through colour charts as the last one left.*

Who is he?

An aardvark in a business suit. The scene came to me when I learnt that the thick-skinned, ant-eating aardvark constantly rearranges its sets.

This could be a way of 'casting' minor characters. They still need to live and breathe on the page even though you don't want to spend too much time developing them. Your task is to write about your character in such as way only you will know where the original idea came from – a moose as X Factor contestant, a gorilla as diplomat, a giraffe as neighbourhood gossip....

PROSE POETRY – A LITERARY CASSEROLE

"I love the swirl and swing of words as they tangle with human emotions"

James Michener

What is prose poetry?

It is a form that uses the lyrical language of poetry but looks like conventional prose on the page with sentences and full stops and all the other hallmarks of a regular passage of writing. It can be of any length from a sentence to a book.

Here's a quote from the King James Bible, sometimes called the longest prose poem ever written:

> *For God hath not given us the spirit of fear; but of power, and of love, and of a sound mind.* Timothy 1:7

I chose this line at random, but it employs a number of important techniques: the repetition builds a compelling rhythm in a 21 words sentence and, while the language is simple – most of the words have one syllable – the meaning is rich and complex. It compares and contrasts a negative with strong positives and it is no coincidence that three positives are put forward. There is something magical about three. It works in design and it works in words as we saw in the section on speech writing.

Here's another example of prose poetry. It is a passage taken from *By Grand Central Station I Laid Down and Wept*, a novella-length prose poem written by Elizabeth Smart in the 1940s about her passionate love affair with a British poet.

The parchment philosopher has no traffic with the night, and no conception of the price of love. With smoky circles of thought he tries to combat the fog, and with anagrams to defeat anatomy. I posture in vain with his weapons, even though I am balmed with his nicotine herbs.

There is a lot of smoking imagery here with the mention of nicotine, fog and smoky circles and I get a picture of long discussions conducted in a blue haze of cigarette smoke. Her critic tries to defeat passion with reasoned argument and I like the way the author uses alliteration to describe cerebral word games combating sexual desire.

These are two rare examples. Prose poetry is usually much, much shorter. American poet and novelist Naomi Shihab Nye thinks of it as pocket-sized literature, stand-alone paragraphs that garnish a page rather than dominating it. One of the advantages, she believes is that while people often say they don't like poetry, no one says they don't like paragraphs.

It is essential that some poetical features are used in a prose poem. Without being told, the reader has to feel that what they reading is something very different from an essay or a story.

One writing tool we haven't explored yet is assonance and its subtlety works particularly well in prose poetry. It's the name given to the repetition of similar or identical vowel sounds in a phrase. For example, the phrase 'I blew the balloon' gives the comical ooo sound.

I've played around with the double ee sound in this line from an imaginary speech:

We need to feed the hungry, to free ourselves from the greed of our own desire that forces us to consume more than we need and strangles good deeds before they are born.

Here is a much more sophisticated example that appears in Edgar Allan Poe's poem *The Raven*.

And the silken sad uncertain rustling of each purple curtain

The assonance is the pUr and cUr sound in the last two words, and there's also a neat visual connection with the other u words in the line – Uncertain and rUstling.

Mean Streets – Martin Scorsese's 1973 film – is also an example of assonance and the title comes from Raymond Chandler: *Down these mean streets a man must go who is not himself mean.*

You could also try a sprinkling of onomatopoeia. This is where the sound of the words expresses the meaning. Music is conveyed through the use of words like hum, clap, twang, jangle, ring, ping, toot, rattle, rap, tap, boom, rattle and plunk. The kitchen is cluttered with onomatopoeia. Food can crackle or sizzle in the pan, and if the oil is too hot it may splatter. Liquids splash or gush if the chef is too hasty and when the meal is served up we may munch, gobble, and crunch. The more delicate may just nibble.

Wilfred Owen gave us the sound of World War I guns in *Anthem for Doomed Youth* when we looked at alliteration. In this Tennyson example, the 19th century poet laureate tries to convey gentler, more complex sounds.

The moan of doves in immemorial elms,
And murmuring of innumerable bees.

You could put that in a contemporary context by describing a cappuccino afternoon perhaps, with no work or school or college making demands. And if you don't have one of those very often, you should.

Or do the opposite and create a cacophony on the page. The word comes from the Greek meaning bad sound and you can do just that by bringing hard, jarring words together – perhaps using short sentences – to describe what? A car crash? A tornado?

What else can we do with sound? There is a link with movement – the hesitant shuffling slippers of an old man, the whoosh of a speeding car. Still with Tennyson, we are back to war, this time in the Crimea in the 1850s.

Half a league, half a league
Half a league onward.

Say it aloud and the emphatic rhythm is the sound of men and horses thundering into a valley.

Tennyson uses anaphora, the literary term for the repetition of a word or phrase at the beginning of lines or, in a prose poem, sentences. Here we can almost hear the roar of the big guns and see the shells flying towards them.

Cannon to right of them,
Cannon to left of them,
Cannon in front of them

Robert Browning wrote *How They Brought The Good News From Ghent To Aix* to give a sense of a horse galloping. (He never bothers to reveal the good news.) Again, you need to read it aloud to get the impact.

Not a word to each other: we kept the great pace--
Neck by neck, stride by stride, never changing our place;
I turned in my saddle and made its girths tight,
Then shortened each stirrup and set the pique right.

In Robert Louis Stevenson's poem for children there is more dash and less rattle than in the average railway carriage. It doesn't remind me of trains as much as it does of children charging across a playground pretending to be trains.

Faster than fairies, faster than witches,
Bridges and houses, hedges and ditches
And charging along like troops in a battle,
All through the meadows, the horses and cattle

We can do anything with words. Who needs mood music and sound effects? Now, you're ready to tackle a prose poem.

EXERCISE

Select a household object – such as a potato peeler or bottle opener – something very familiar that you can hold in your hands. Do you remember where you bought it? Perhaps it was left over after a party or it somehow migrated from your parents' house to your kitchen cupboard. Does the way it look or smell or feel remind you of something else?

Turn it into a metaphor. Here's my example:

The old dressmaking scissors have orange pantaloons for handles.

Or an extended simile:

The scissors were like a tall Spanish gentleman, out of fashion and faintly ridiculous with the plastic handles taking on the shape of billowing orange pantaloons.

Add any memories or associations this object triggers – it could be about people or places, it could be about something you've experienced or a story you've heard.

You should now have a collection of notes. Turn it into a coherent passage of writing using some of the tools we have explored already – personification, varied sentence construction, humour, sensory description, concrete imagery...

A prose poem is permission to let your imagination loose.

LOL FOR BEGINNERS

"Any fool with steady hands and a working set of lungs can build up a house of cards and then blow it down, but it takes a genius to make people laugh"

Stephen King

I've already explained why I think humour is important to writers of any genre and the following exercises will explore two comedic devices – understatement and reversal. Both are often considered to be elements of irony, a type of humour sometimes described as quintessentially British. It may be, but it is not exclusively British, as these examples show.

UNDERSTATEMENT

It has to have three essential ingredients:

1. **It has to be accurate.** If you have a character saying a meal wasn't bad, the food has to have been a gastronomic wonder.
2. **The reader has to have expectations** – otherwise you can't upset them. You may have problems if specialist knowledge is required to appreciate what is happening.
3. **There has to be a moment of surprise.** As in: It was thrilling, it was nerve tingling, it was quite nice. Or the subject matter itself will create the surprise. Jeeves, the deadpan butler in P.G Wodehouse's classic Bertie Wooster series when asked for an

opinion on William Shakespeare replied that the playwright seemed to have given *uniform satisfaction.*

Litotes is the literary term for a dramatic understatement and a famous example comes from one of my favourite poems *To My Coy Mistress* written by Andrew Marvel, the puritan MP for Hull in Cromwell's government. The poem uses a wealth of literary devices with a skill that is so precise it almost makes you cry. Or perhaps that's just me.

It has a universal and timeless theme, not love but lust. A man is trying to persuade a woman into his bed. One of the arguments he uses is that you are a long time dead or, as Marvell put it in this understatement:

*The grave's a fine and private place
But none I think do there in embrace*

Here's an old joke that has the same qualities:

A husband comes home from work to find his wife being chased around the kitchen by a murderer with a large axe. The man assesses the situation and asks, "Shall I get my own dinner then, dear?"

And from real life:

The great newspaper journalist William Connor who wrote under the name Cassandra returned to the Daily Mirror after active service in WWII. His first column after his return began with, "As I was saying before I was so rudely interrupted..."

And finally, this gem re-surfaces on the internet whenever there is terrorist threat. I haven't been able to find the author but it can serve as a model for the technique.

The British have raised their security level from 'Miffed' to 'Peeved.' Soon, though, security levels may be raised yet again to 'Irritated' or even 'A Bit Cross.' Brits have not been 'A Bit Cross' since the Blitz in 1940 when tea supplies all but ran out.

Look for other examples in conversation and on television. It's all around us.

EXERCISE I
Find your subject. That's the tough part.

Listen to the news, read a newspaper, discover the commanding stories of the last week, the ones everyone's heard about (remember you need your reader/audience to have certain assumptions about what you will say.)

Try describing any recent political event as a casual understatement or write a short story around an old joke (you don't have to go further than the internet to search for your material).

REVERSAL
This is a simple device that has been the basis of numerous comedy sketches, sitcoms, books and films. The reader or audience is presented with a situation or a character that goes against the normal order.

Shakespeare was fond of the technique. He used it when he has his leading female character pretend to be a man for much of the play; when Tatiana, the Queen of the Fairies falls in love with Bottom, who is not only a rough yokel with a big ego, but also has a donkey's head. Jane Austen uses it in *Emma* when Harriet has to give the heroine advice about love and marriage.

A contemporary and very obvious example is *The Simpsons* (where most forms of humour can be found). Daughter Lisa is not only clever and knowledgeable; she also has far more sophisticated tastes than her parents while still being a little girl.

However, in any league table first place has to go the classic and much loved example of Jack Lemon in *Some Like It Hot*. While dressed as a woman, Lemon has been dating a millionaire. In the final scene of the film he has to explain why they can't marry. He gives several reasons: they won't get along, the millionaire's mother will disapprove, they won't be able to have children and, finally, he delivers the absolute clincher by taking off his wig and declaring, "I'm a man!"

The audience knows what's coming – some explosion of shock, outrage, bewilderment. Not a bit of it. In a heartbeat and a half Osgood Fielding III delivers the punch line: "Nobody's perfect." And we've been saying it to each other ever since.

EXERCISE II

Write a scene using the reversal device involving one of these pairs

- A student and a teacher
- A voter and a political representative
- A fan and a celebrity

Bring the two together in a situation that the reader is used to – a fan asking for an autograph, for example – and then go off in another direction.

My feeling is that the humour is best revealed in dialogue rather than through description. You could write it as though it were a script. Many websites will give you guidance about formatting a script for different mediums (theatre, radio, film etc) and there is also software available, but don't get bogged in that now.

Instead fold a sheet of paper in half lengthways so you have two equal columns: the first column is for the names of the characters and in the second column is the dialogue – it works fine as long as you keep the dialogue confined to the second column.

Concentrate on being funny: you can work on the finer points of script layout later, once you've made someone laugh.

THE HORROR!
THE HORROR!

"[Horror fiction] shows us that the control we believe we have is purely illusory, and that every moment we teeter on chaos and oblivion"

Clive Barker

Karl Albrecht writing in *Psychology Today* in March 2012 described five basic fears from which all our other fears stem.

Extinction – fear of annihilation, of ceasing to exist. The most basic and the most universal, but it also includes a range of more specific fears, such as a fear of heights.
Mutilation – including the fear of being invaded, taken over. It also includes phobias about animals and insects.
Loss of Autonomy – fear of being paralyzed, restricted, imprisoned, smothered – physically or emotionally
Separation – fear of being lost, abandoned, rejected, fear of losing respect
Ego-death because the worst thing that can happen to us isn't always something we can touch or see, but how it make us feel. This includes fear of disgrace, shame, of being unworthy, unlovable.

Stories often combine a number of these basic fears: *The Blair Witch Project* – the surprise breakthrough film of 1999 and still one of the

THE HORROR! THE HORROR!

most successful independent films of all time – deals with a primitive fear that we have all experienced, getting lost.

The theme of Robert Louis Stevenson's *Dr Jekyll and Mr Hyde* is ego death. The part of ourselves that we like, the nice part that can tell a joke and be a good friend, the sensible part that works reasonably hard and does more or less what is expected (like not knocking old ladies over in the street), is taken over by our uncontrolled wilder nature which only cares about one thing: self, self, self.

That's the core material we are working with as writers, but to create genuine fear the story has to be real to the reader. That's not the same as saying that it is has to be realistic. You can allow your imagination to roam free, looting fairy tales and fables for inspiration, creating dystopic tomorrows and fantasy worlds. However, bear in mind that one of the most important elements that distinguishes fiction from real life is that in fiction things happen for a reason.

That's one of the points Susan Hill makes about writing ghost stories. Author of probably the most successful modern ghost story *The Woman in Black*, she says that in fiction the ghost must have a reason to appear. It may be seeking revenge or want the truth to be uncovered; it could even be altruistic and want to warn the living, but the ghost has to have a motive for appearing because without it you may have a ghost, but you haven't got a story.

When writing a horror story without paranormal elements, choose something you are afraid of and try the "what if…?" approach.

A bit icky about the things that live in the flower bed? Think of the slugs in Shaun Hutson's novel of the same name eating anything that gets in their way, including people. Read *Cuckoo* by Julia Crouch if you've ever been nervous about a controlling best friend taking over.

Or consider a social problem and add your own twist. What if you had a violent boyfriend and all your friends thought he was wonderful? This is the subject of Elizabeth Haynes' first novel *Into the Darkest Corner* and, although it is firmly in the crime fiction genre, any writer wanting to scare readers should have a well-thumbed copy on his or her bookshelf.

Push the idea as far as it will possibly go, but before you start to write read this poem by Emily Dickinson.

One need not be a chamber to be haunted,
One need not be a house;
The brain has corridors surpassing
Material place.

Far safer, of a midnight meeting
External ghost,
Than an interior confronting
That whiter host.

Far safer through an Abbey gallop,
The stones achase,
Than, moonless, one' s own self encounter
In lonesome place.

Ourself, behind ourself concealed,
Should startle most;
Assassin, hid in our apartment,
Be horror' s least.

The prudent carries a revolver,
He bolts the door,
O' erlooking a superior spectre
More near.

EXERCISE

My final horror writing exercise comes with a health warning. Students have told me that they've had nightmares after completing it in class.

Jot down somewhere you personally (not a character – YOU) feel safe and secure. Maybe it's even a bit dull. It could be the local library, at home in bed, driving along the coast road singing a duet with the radio...

Next shut your eyes and select at random one of the five fears listed in *Psychology Today*. Pick up your pen. Your task is to find some way of connecting the fear and the situation. If you can scare yourself you know your reader is going to be terrified.

Your combination could look something like this:

Bed and Fear of Separation
Your main character wakes up and everyone has gone. Mum, Dad, younger brother, cat. No warning. No note. The neighbours don't know anything. The car has gone, but all their phones are still at home. And then there's a noise...

Favourite café and Loss of Autonomy
A demonstration is planned, but the main character is unaware as s/he sips a double shot espresso to clear a hangover. Through the café window, he or she notices police in riot gear and soon after gas is released and seeps into the coffee shop. Everyone is coughing, choking, in distress, but only the main character is paralysed. Only the main character realises that something very strange is happening as s/he is carried away by someone who is most definitely not a doctor...

Go for it. If you can't sleep tonight you can always turn all the lights on and write.

NO ONE GETS TIRED OF ONCE UPON A TIME

"The fact is that writing is hard work, and sometimes you don't want to do it, and you can't think of what to write next, and you're fed up with the whole damn business. Do you think plumbers don't feel like that about their work from time to time? Of course there will be days when the stuff is not flowing freely. What you do then is MAKE IT UP"

Philip Pullman

As soon as a toddler walks she dances. As soon as she can hold a crayon she draws pictures and as soon as she has words she wants stories. Pretty soon she will make her own stories. Don't wait to find a subject that inspires you. Inspiration is more likely to come if you have a pen in your hand or your fingers are already tapping away at the keyboard. James Kelman the Scottish writer who won the Booker Prize in 1994 with *How Late It Was, How Late*, has a foolproof method of beating writer's block.

Just write.

Write when you can – even when your head feels empty and your imagination has gone on holiday Even if all you can write is: I don't know what to write and I don't know why I'm sitting here. Your brain doesn't like a vacuum, something will come.

Inspiration rises from strange corners of the mind that can't be switched on with a click of the fingers. It lies in half-remembered shreds of conversation you had with a school friend aged 11, the sight of a man with a pony tail crying as he waits for a train and noticing that a leather belt is buckled around a child's swing in the playground. It comes from being open to these thoughts and observations and it's also about remembering old stories and having the confidence to tell them again in a new way.

Here's one of the world's oldest stories.

A father has two sons. The family have some money and the younger son asks for his share of his inheritance and leaves home. He lives a wild, irresponsible life, cutting himself off from his family. The older son stays at home, working in his father's business. Eventually the younger son runs out of money. He tries to support himself but it is hard to get even the lowest paid job and there are times he goes hungry. It is then that he decides to go home because he knows that even the most junior person in his father's business has a better life than he has. The father is delighted to see him and welcomes him back, but the older son is angry and complains that all his hard work and loyalty count for nothing. His father says that he does appreciate everything he's done but he is happy because now his youngest son is back where he belongs.

You may have recognised the Prodigal Son, one of Christ's parables told in the Gospel of St Luke, but versions have been around for thousands of years because it touches on core issues in family life. There is a similar story in Jewish scripture and in Buddhist writings.

EXERCISE

Think about using the Prodigal Son as the basis of a contemporary short story.

You could change the gender – mother and daughters. Perhaps ditch the rich element and concentrate on the emotional commitment and set it within a specific culture – Irish/Jewish/Greek/Black/New Age Travellers/Martians – whatever interests you.

Where to start? When the young son leaves? When he comes home? Does the young son stay at home or he is off again with more family money in his pockets? Perhaps you could start your story when the father dies.

How to start? With dialogue? With a dramatic event? With description?

Whose side are you on? This is your story. If you are rooting for the older brother you might want to write it from his first person point of view. Or maybe you want the reader to make up their own mind and your third person narrator is someone in the father's business – the not-quite-neutral outsider as in *The Great Gatsby* or *Wuthering Heights*.

You don't have to follow the original story slavishly... use it as a starting point and see where it takes you.

Surfing through Amazon will show that other authors have started in the same place. Don't let that put you off.

Home by Marilynne Robinson won the Orange Prize for her story about two adult children returning to their father's house: one is a resentful daughter nursing her father and the other is the son who left in disgrace 20 years earlier.

Home by Nobel prize winner Toni Morrison is about an African American soldier returning from the Korea War who doesn't want to go home but discovers he has to in order to save his sister.

There's room for all these stories because you can make the old new: you can make it yours. And no one else could write it the way you can.

EVERYTHING HAPPENS SOMEWHERE

"I wanted to paint a picture that people would stand before and forget that it was made of paint. I wanted it to creep into them like a bar of music and mushroom there like a soft bullet"

O. Henry

Choose somewhere you know well – somewhere you visited often or lived. I suggest you don't choose where you are living now as you'll have more freedom to be creative if there is some emotional and physical distance.

The place can be inside or outside, it's up to you. It could be a school playground or a shop, a river valley, or a kitchen that was once yours. This exercise is in two parts, but you can spread the work out over a week or so. In fact, it might help if you do because sometimes you need ideas to ferment.

EXERCISE PART I
If you are outside....

Write from the perspective of a bird circulating overhead and then coming into land. You're not literally a bird or a plane or superman (unless you want to be) what you are doing is giving the reader a wide overview and then you drill down to the smaller details.

It might be easier to think of it as a camera shot. First we see a city nestling in a valley, we move in to see the parks and factories, the roads slashing across the landscape, the rows of houses, closer still, we see the reflection on the school windows, closer still we can smell the rubbery tarmac in the sports field....

If you are inside...

Go for detail: the ornaments on the mantelpiece, the ticking of a clock, the paint on the wall. Try writing from different perspectives: a small child sitting on the floor would notice things that a prospective house purchaser wouldn't see who, in turn, could detect faults that might pass by the bored teenage longing to leave home.

EXERCISE PART II

You have started with a real place, somewhere you know intimately, now something happens in that place, now it becomes a work of fiction.

I suggest you take your notes and go somewhere that takes you away from your usual writing routine. University researchers believe that a busy cafe is probably ideal. The buzz of conversation and the background burble of coffee-making machines drowns out distracting sounds and because you've brought your laptop or notebook it's a public statement that you are there to write so you are more likely to stay focused. It worked for J.K. Rowling. She wrote a lot of the first Harry Potter book at The Elephant House café on George IV Bridge in Edinburgh.

However, if you normally write in a café go to a different one in a different part of town, or change the time you go, or where you sit. If all else fails, you can now have a virtual coffee shop piped to your shed/writing room/corner of the bedroom because the clever people at Coffitvity (http://www.coffitivity.com) have acted on the research results. By clicking on their website you can have the sound track of a bustling café wherever you are.

EVERYTHING HAPPENS SOMEWHERE

I tried it out but it didn't mask my granddaughter's laughter from the floor above and the faint rumble from the washing machine on the floor below. The trouble with home grown background noise is that it belongs to me and threatens to make demands at any moment. Physically removing yourself from home is at least part of the reason cafes can be creative places and, of course, Coffitivity can't deliver the smell of strong coffee. Still, if you can't get out, you might like to try it and see if it works from you.

Where ever you choose to write, you already have a setting so half the work is done. It needs a story to bring it to life, but the place you've chosen can also add an important quality by reflecting the underlying theme. This a useful device for horror writers, but it is one the rest of us can apply as well. The physical setting could mirror the personalities of the main characters. I'm thinking of Annie Proulx's *Shipping News* where Newfoundland's rough strength is tested again and again by elements it is powerless to change while the isolation of the ranch in Steinbeck's *Of Mice and Men* allows us to see the bleakness of George Milton and Lennie Small's lives.

The setting can also provide a contrast to the conflict that dominates the storyline. The Shire in *Lord of the Rings* represents the values that would be destroyed if Sauron prevailed and the country house in *Howard's End* reinforces the human qualities of nurture, love and respect that can be trampled on when cold logic and hard-headed business sense is allowed to rule. A place can prepare the reader for the story that is about to unfold by conveying a sense of unease from the start and, of course, it can be a character in its own right: Hogwarts, for instance.

So...what kind of story would match or contrast with the place you have described?

- A zombie attack in a High Street where most of the shops are boarded up.
- A man falls in love and a woman doesn't in a kitchen that smells of wet washing and fried bacon.
- A ghost roams the corridors of a cold, intimidating school

- Once it is dark the tools in a shed come alive in a creative huddle of wood shavings and paint.
- A serial killer moves in next door to a chaotic household of boisterous dogs and children where the month's salary only lasts three weeks and Mum and Dad still like each other.

Choose one of these ideas or find one of your own that you really want to write about. Make the place and the story fit together, the place supporting the story, adding something to it.

Start writing even if you don't know where it will go. And smell the coffee.

RULES TO THE RIGHT, RULES TO THE LEFT

"Far better to write twaddle or anything, anything, than nothing at all"

Katherine Mansfield

In this exercise you're going to write a lipogram. You might want to mention that casually on facebook or during a telephone conversation: what did I do yesterday? Knocked off a few lipograms, just for practice, just to keep my hand in....

The word comes yet again from the Ancient Greek and for once its original meaning hasn't been distorted by the passing of time. It meant then what it means today: leaving out a letter. There is an 1819 example in the rare books section of my local library. It's a collection of sermons by a preacher in Rome who couldn't pronounce Rs so everything he said and wrote avoided that awkward letter. History doesn't record how he coped when asked his address.

By now, you're probably asking why.

Writers often test themselves by applying self-imposed rules. Poets thrive on them. A sonnet, for example, has 14 lines and the first eight will usually pose a question, the turning point comes at line nine and then the next seven lines answers the question...and all in rhyme.

Prose writers have it easier, other than following the conventions of punctuation and grammar (apart from the times we choose to ignore them for artistic reasons), length is usually the only restriction. Well, for some that is just too easy.

In 1939 Ernest Vincent Wright self-published *Gadsby*, a 50,000 word novel that doesn't contain the letter "e", the most common letter in the English language. First editions are now worth a lot of money, as the print run was small, it was not reviewed and the author died shortly after it was published so he wasn't around to promote it. It did, however, became sought after following the publication of a much more serious French novel in the late 1960s that also shunned the letter "e" – Georges Perec's *La Dispartion*. By the way, "e" is even more common in French than it is in English. Perec's parents were Polish Jews who immigrated to France in the 1920s. His soldier father was killed in 1940 while his mother died in a concentration camp. Some critics suggest that Perec's novel-length lipogram should be seen as a metaphor for the holocaust. It was translated into English in 1995 under the title *A Void*. (Perec also wrote a novel in the 1970s that only contained words that use the vowel e – he joked that he had a lot going spare.)

You may now be thinking all well and good, but I am not the kind of writer that enjoys literary masochism. And frankly neither am I. While I can see the point in striving to create a work of art like a sonnet, extraordinary limitations on prose are not going to produce a more compelling story, a more evocative memoir or a more vivid passage of description.

BUT

You knew there would be a but, didn't you? This without-the-e-word exercise is another way of extracting yourself from a rut. The very fact you can't use THE will mean you will have to re-think every sentence.

And we do need rules. One of the worst things you can say to a writer is you can write about anything you like and it doesn't matter how long it is. And, by the way, there's no deadline. If no one else will impose rules and deadlines, we have to make them up for ourselves.

I'm a slow writer by inclination, but one of the easiest and quickest passages of writing I have ever completed was for an exhibition on the theme of shoes. I knew it would be part of a live performance and I was told it also had to fit on one side of A4 because of printing constraints. The organiser stressed she preferred something light and amusing, adding that I could write about anything I liked as long it was shoe-related, but it would really help if somehow it explained the exhibition's title *Quince Pies* because ...it's probably easier to show you what I wrote.

A Perfect Pair

Say it slowly, say it softly: quince pies. Now a little louder, more throat less voice.

Quince Pies

In Spanish it means 15 feet and it was in Andalusia that we met. A lone voice sang flamenco while a ceiling fan stirred hot air. Swing doors swung and I saw him. There was 15 feet between us: the distance between passion and desire.

He wasn't tall in the way heroes are supposed to be tall in the stories that no one reads twice. And he wasn't as young as he should have been. But when he turned to greet me I drowned in eyes the colour of rain.

I was wearing new shoes. Shoes that cupped my toes in an embrace of buttery suede; shoes that clinched my ankles in a dominant excess of colour. Shoes that chastised my sole with the iron brawn of unforgiving leather.

And did I mention the heels? They were empire heels. Empire State.

They were shoes to die for. And they were killing me.

When I walked I wobbled and when I wobbled I winced. Quince pies is a long, long way in new shoes.

The man I wanted as my forever lover turned, looked down and smiled.

"I love your arches," he purred.

"Foot fetishist?" I asked, raising an eyebrow. He nodded.

"Masochist," he said. It wasn' t a question.

EXERCISE

Ok, your turn. You know how you are going to write: without words that contain the letter e. And you're going to write about a walk in the country. It might have been a walk you went on this morning when you left your front door or it might be a memory from years ago. You can't have trees I'm afraid, but you can have oak and larch, but not alder, cedar or elm. No lake but you can have a pond, no lane but path is just fine. Flowers are out but there is room for grass

You might think that there can't be anything worse than managing without THE but past tense – the default tense for story telling – becomes tricky. You can have was and said, of course, but you can't have any word ending in ed.

So maybe this exercise is the time to play around with the present tense. (It used to be said that the present tense only worked well over short distances – the essay, the short story and in flash fiction – but this was before Hilary Mantle wrote *Wolf Hall*, all 650 pages of it.)

This is the kind of exercise you can do again and again when you've finished the crossword and there's nothing good on television, when on a train journey or sitting in a dentist's waiting room. Choose a different subject each time and off you go.

Trust me. It's fun. Really.

RHYME TIME

"Imaginary gardens with real toads in them"
Marianne Moore's definition of poetry

This first section is a warm up. After that you're doing grown up poetry, the real stuff.

Think of an object. It can be as ordinary as you like. Next think of an image that goes with it and put the two together in one line.

My object was a red flower on a patio and because it was red and it stood out, it made me think of a flag.

> *A flapping red flag grew out of the flower plot*

Write a line on the same subject but this time it must have 10 syllables – no more and no less.

> *A raw red flag grew in the flower pot*

Next write two or three lines where the sense runs on and there is a full stop in the middle of lines. Don't worry about syllables.

> *In the flower pot a flag of a flower*
> *grew. It flapped its raw redness*
> *across the broken concrete.*

Now – two lines that rhyme and each must have 10 syllables

In the flower pot a raw red flag grew
its bloody petals pearled by the dew

EXERCISE
Practice over...Write a poem made up of six rhyming couplets (so 12 lines in all) and each line must have 10 syllables.

Subject
Choose something you like that perhaps other people wouldn't see as immediately lovable or even suitable as a subject for a poem. So, not the red flower I wrote about, but the open bag of fertiliser in the shed...

There is nothing off limits for a poet. The Irish poet Patrick Kavanagh wrote a sonnet to the hospital ward where he was treated for lung cancer. Chilean poet and politician Pablo Neruda published an entire collection that praises the ordinary – such as socks. The award-winning American poet Sharon Olds writes with great frankness about sex and the body and the corners of life that are often neglected. Among other things, she has celebrated tampons and toilets in her work.

Rhyming Advice
Don't select a word just because it rhymes and avoid the obvious like cat and mat, June and moon. However, having said that, don't despise short, ordinary words either. What could you make out of night and skies, bright and eyes? It might not sound that promising, yet Byron crafted some of the most beautiful lines in the English language with those end rhymes

She walks in beauty, like the night
Of cloudless climes and starry skies,
And all that's best of dark and bright
Meets in her aspect and her eyes;

Work hard at making it appear as though you chose the rhyming words because you wanted them and no others and hey! it's a lucky coincidence that they happen to rhyme.

RHYME TIME

There are many print and online rhyming dictionaries you can use for inspiration. I came up with 256 rhymes for WRITE in a matter of minutes. My favourite were height, bullfight, plebiscite and hermaphrodite.

Some people feel that it's cheating to use a dictionary, but I heard Leonard Cohen in a radio interview say that he often picked one up, not necessarily to check for a particular rhyme, but to read through it like a book, immersing himself in the language of rhyme. If it's good enough for Leonard Cohen...

MAGIC FOR GROWN UPS

"Logic only gives man what he needs...magic gives him what he wants"

Tom Robbins

Magic Realism is a literary genre where extraordinary and magical things happen but – and this is probably the defining quality – the characters in the story treat them as everyday reality. Nowadays we tend to associate the term with literature from Latin American where the phrase translates to marvellous reality which may be a better way of thinking about it. However, there are many writers around the world who are creating remarkable stories through mixing the ordinary with the fantastic.

If you are new to this genre here's a very partial list of novels and short story collections that will take you to places where anything can happen.

Nights at the Circus Angela Carter
One Hundred Years of Solitude by Gabriel Garcia Marrquez
The House of the Spirits by Isabel Allende,
Sexing the Cherry by Jeanette Winterson
The Book of Sand by Jorge Luis Borges
Midnight's Children by Salman Rushdi
Life of Pi by Yann Matel

A film to look out for is *Being John Malkovich*. Made in 1999, it contains as many surprises at the end as it does in the beginning. I won't spoil the plot, but it starts with a puppeteer working as a filing clerk on floor seven and a half of a Manhattan office building. He and his colleagues have to bend over, because the ceiling is only about five feet high, but no one seems to notice. Once we accept this it's not such a stretch to discover that the puppeteer finds a doorway into the brain of actor John Malkovich.

Writers in the past have also blurred the line between reality and fantasy. The Russian author Gogol wrote a short story in the 1830s about a nose that took off and started its own career and Swift wrote *Gulliver's Travels* a hundred years earlier. An immediate success, it has never been out of print since and it's worth re-reading, especially if you've only read the children's abridged version.

EXERCISE
Choose a character:

- Hospital doctor in an accident and emergency department
- Religious leader just about to make a sermon
- Gang leader with revenge on his mind
- Harassed teacher with a difficult class

What happens:

Your character feels an irritating itch around the shoulder blades. There's an overwhelming need to scratch. It gets worse. He or she just has to scratch again. And again. Finally, your character finds a mirror and sees that wings are beginning to sprout.

What kind of wings? Magnificent archangel's wings, the kind you might see in a medieval painting; soft, downy cherub wings belonging to a baby angel, translucent fairy wings?

Or perhaps they have the arching beauty of a swan or a condor? The iridescence of a kingfisher or the night time wings of a raven? Or could they belong to a scrawny pigeon, a wasp or a creature from the supernatural world (and not in a good way)? You could even have aircraft wings – one student came up with that idea.

What does your character do with their newly acquired wings? Shrug and get on with life, hide or soar into the clouds...?

That's not the story. That's the start. The story is what happens next.

This is a classic creative writing exercise – certainly not original to me – but it seems to plug into a powerful human desire that hasn't been quenched by the aviation industry. Think of all the stories we have about flying from Icarus in Greek mythology to Harry Potter playing quidditch. See where the idea takes you and remember to include gritty, ordinary detail about the humdrum world that your character inhabits.

And fly....

WHAT'S THE WORST THAT COULD HAPPEN?

"The simplest questions are the most difficult"
William S. Burroughs

Journalists ask five questions:

- Who is the story about?
- What happened?
- When did it take place?
- Where did it take place?
- Why did it happen?

Creative writers ask: what if...?

They can also ask: what's the worst that could happen?

We don't write stories about nice, well-balanced people with secure, worthwhile jobs who were brought up by nice, well-balanced parents and go on to marry someone who leads a similar quiet and untroubled life. We don't live lives like that. Stuff happens. And it's the stuff that creates a story

Raymond Chandler, creator of hard-boiled crime and mystery fiction, advised letting a gun go off whenever a story stalled. He found it stopped a scene from dragging. Asking what's the worst that could happen might be your way of firing a bullet.

What's the worst that could happen in a creative writing class?

Cathy Dreyer explores just that subject in a story that I discovered on her blog *Write a Novel in 10 minutes Flat* – a title that has its tongue firmly in its cheek (http://writeanovelin10minutesflat.wordpress. com). Cathy is a poet who has had work broadcast on BBC Radio Four, but before reading her amusing and ever-so-slightly worrying take on the subject I want to look at a way you could brain storm story ideas when you are working on your own. If you are in a class or with a group of friends ideas can ping across the room and spark several more, but when you are on your own a spider diagram can work just as well.

Spider diagrams are very similar to Mind Maps – invented by Tony Buzan – but you don't need a bag of felt tip pens before you start and the diagram can be laid out anyway that suits you and the subject best. I know that a lot of people find that introducing images and having fun with multi-coloured wavy lines is an aid to creativity, but I think there's a danger of it turning into yet another way of avoiding the one thing that you desperately want to do, the thing you bought this book to do, and that is write. Top American blogger Leo Babauta says, writers should not even be called writers: "putting things off-ists" would be more accurate.

We want to write more than anything else, but instead we surf ebay or watch other people's stories on television and dream about the ones we would write if only we had the time. I know writers who bake cakes as a deadline approaches. At any other time shop-bought is just fine for their families, but when they know they have to write, when there is no way of escaping it, they decide that their little ones deserve an Esterházy torte. They get over it – the ones who write properly, the ones who are published – even if it means whisking chocolate butter cream at 3pm and polishing the final full stop at 3am. However, when it comes to spider diagrams and finding ways of generating ideas, I suggest we play safe and put the colour pencils away.

WHAT'S THE WORST THAT COULD HAPPEN?

I realise I may be explaining the very, very obvious as spider diagrams and mind maps are used throughout industry and education, but here is how I suggest you do it.

Work quickly. Give yourself a strict deadline. 10 minutes maximum.

Get a blank piece of paper – A3 would be nice as it would give you so much room to write, but A4 works well and has the advantage of being notebook size. You can stick it in later.

Turn the paper around and work landscape. Write the subject in the middle. Draw a nice big bubble around it. From that bubble draw lines that end in idea bubbles and from those ideas come more lines and more bubbles that indicate sub plots and possible events.

The informality of the map says that these ideas don't have to be well thought out and properly structured – at this stage they are just ideas. Anything goes. And because this is a very personal tool, there's no reason it has to make sense to anyone else. If the phrase *Auntie Lou-Lou's birthday* is shorthand for major disaster then write it in.

One of the reasons I like spider diagrams is the way that ideas can be seen in a glance – that and the fact it's not a list. A list imposes an order, but spider diagrams are notes without a hierarchy. With a spider diagram you don't have to make a decision until you're good and ready to make a decision.

And now a story about the creative writing student from hell.

BACK TO CREATIVE WRITING SCHOOL

From the desk of James Sneathe
By Cathy Dreyer

High Poot House, High Poot-On-Chester, IB 2RT

Mr B. Thompson, MA.
Head of Creative Writing,
Dept of Literary Fulfilment,
University of Polchester,
Polchester, PC1 4YY.

Dear Brian,

After everything that's happened, I feel the very least I owe you is a full explanation. You'll have had my formal letter of apology via the Dean's office, of course. It was written by the lawyers and scarcely offers much insight into what took place. With all hopes of meeting you in person finally dashed by my ban, 'in perpetuity', no less, from the university, its premises and personnel, I am writing to you, and perhaps that's appropriate.

Whilst I take full responsibility for my conduct, please believe that my motivation was only ever to win your approval for my work. I was tremendously struck by what you said about the importance of impact, surprise and theatre in the opening of a story. And more so by your remarks about the competition we novelists (and would-be novelists!!) face from today's 'multi-media, multi-channel world'.

But I confess, when it came to it, I was stumped. I spent the first three days inventing reasons not to write and the following three in bed with a high temperature. So it was already late on the eve of your class when I finally felt able to gather my thoughts and put pen to paper. (Or, more properly in this day and age, fingertips to computer keyboard.)

'Dazzle me,' you said. But all my 'bright' ideas seemed dull. I had nothing, no spark, let alone a flame. Doubt snuffed out every glimmering idea. Then, quite suddenly, it came to me: laughter, my

140

old friend in adversity! (I am rather known for my sense of humour, as you may have gathered from my contributions in class.) I thought, if nothing else, I'll raise my flagging spirits on one of the many jocular cyber websites out there.

When I saw the gag on Wikilarfs it seemed like the answer. It had everything. All the elements you asked for and more. Granted it was an unorthodox approach, but, as you have often said, the best stories exist *between* the lines, rather than on them. Furthermore, you did not stipulate the homework must be written. I checked.

I am sure you are very angry about what happened. Disciplinary procedures are never pleasant. But I know you to be a man of integrity which means you will not have allowed emotion to cloud your critical faculties. I am, therefore, convinced you'll admit the title of my work *did* surprise you, thus fulfilling at least one of the criteria. Hurrah for me.

It was rather daring and original, wasn't it? I flatter myself that you'll never before have received an assignment headed: 'Just what you always wanted, a man with a very large cock!'

What incalculably bad luck that your computer failed to downlift the accompanying photomontage because of its formation. I experienced a flush of pure, icy horror, when I realised what must have happened. I do absolutely see that the title *on its own* appears odd, if not downright disturbing. Once again, I am sorry.

If only you'd been able to see the picture. Things would have been so different. Any concerns about obscenity, or homophobia, would have been instantly dispelled. Who, really, could be offended by the sight of a man with a large *bird*? (I'm taking it as read that we're all grown-up enough, and yet not too deathly adult, to find a little *double-entendre* more than a small bit funny.)

If all that weren't bad enough, it was still worse luck for us both, that the word 'cock' tripped the university's obscenity sensors (how do they cope on the agriculture courses?) and the whole lot was automatically emailed to the boys in blue. I'll never understand how the detectives ended up back on Wikilarfs, where elements from the less pleasant nooks of the cyber system had replaced the original, charming and hilarious picture, with something more obvious.

Ah, well. It makes a great story anyway. In retrospect, I mean. Now the embarrassment of having to explain the whole sorry affair to the university authorities is over. And now your position is safe, despite the best efforts of Polchester's very own friends of Dorothy.

I still don't understand why my *intention* counted for so little with their kangaroo court, sorry, executive committee. How could they say that the humour (do they even know what the word means?) 'was peculiar to a homophobic context' because it oughtn't to be funny that some men enjoy 'relations' with other men who are well-endowed? Women are always harping on about 'size' and no one pillories them, do they?

As for accusing you of fostering 'a hegemonic ethos and environment in which students felt relaxed about submitting homophobic material'!? What's wrong with students feeling relaxed? (How fortunate that so many of your students who are that way inclined spoke up so forcefully on your behalf. Probably the fact that you're not married and have no children helped 'confound the enemy'.)

To close, I hope that this letter has given you a more complete understanding of the mindset which informed my behaviour and that, now all's told, you won't remember me too unkindly. I'd like to think that you have accepted my apologies with no hard feelings.

For my part, I'm very sorry I won't have the benefit of your wisdom any longer, but I'm sure you'll be glad to hear that, nothing daunted, I intend to continue nurturing my talent and pursuing my dream of publication. As you have often said, 'Writing is carrying on writing.' So, I'm researching courses elsewhere.

Yours sincerely,

Jimbo Sneathe
James 'Jimbo' Sneathe, Esq.,

WHAT'S THE WORST THAT COULD HAPPEN?

PS I trust you had hard copies of your novel and the other files. Plod surely takes first prize for that particular technological snafu. One for the Police Complaints Authority, perhaps?

PPS I've given up trying to send this as an email, there appears to be some kind of bar to communications your end.

© 2013 Cathy Dreyer

Now over to you. I've put a list of ideas below. Choose one and put it in the centre of your paper. Whether you are going for humour or something deep and serious your writing can't be timid. Push the boundaries and then push them a little further.

WHAT'S THE WORST THAT COULD HAPPEN WHEN:

- Registering a death
- Buying a wedding present
- Going for a job interview
- Losing your purse/wallet
- Meeting a parent for lunch

Be big, be bold, be wrong even, but above all be brave.

WHAT'S THE WORST THAT COULD HAPPEN TO YOU AS A WRITER?

I think you know without me having to say a word.

END OF YEAR ASSESSMENT (don't worry – you're doing the assessing)

Write a book review

Book reviewing is an efficient combination of writing and reading. The process of collecting your thoughts together and reflecting on why you liked/loathed something will help you become a better reader of your own writing. There are now plenty of places to submit a review depending on where you live. Here are some of them:

www.amazon.co.uk
www.amazon.com
www.amazon.ca
www.amazon.in
www.waterstones.com/waterstonesweb
www.google.co.uk/googlebooks/mylibrary
www.goodreads.com
www.librarything.com
www.barnesandnoble.com

END OF YEAR ASSESSMENT

Say what you think: then say why you think it
The why is the difficult part to write and the most interesting part to read. Working out why you've formed an opinion about a book shows that you are reading like a writer.

Length
On Amazon anything over 20 words is a review and that's not a bad standard because Awesome! or Rubbish! really won't do.

Word counts are good for writers so I suggest between 50 and 150 words. No, I don't suggest it, this is my last chance to lay down the law so I say it must be between 50 and 150 words (and naturally you'll remember everything I've said about not following rules all the time). But that is a pretty good length to test your ability to write tight, to get your point across while making every word earn its place.

Think of it as a piece of creative flash non-fiction.

What to include
A bit about you, but only if it's relevant. This is debatable, but to my mind there's no getting away from the fact that a review is a personal opinion. While readers don't need to know that you're married with four children and read for 20 minutes every day on the train, it would be useful to reveal that you have a scientific background if you are querying the accuracy of a physics text book.

Fiction
Imagine that you are writing for someone who is very like you.

1. Start with a short outline of the story that doesn't give too much away. Two sentences max – this is not a book report – and you might be able to do it in less. Synopsis writing is a valuable skill and one you will need if you ever consider publication yourself, but it's not easy so the more practice you get the better.

2. Think about the atmosphere – how did the writer make you feel? If the main character is memorable pin down what brought them to life on the page. Dialogue? Description? Consider the novel's weaknesses. Decide if they are enough to put you off reading another

book by the same author. For example, I happen to think the plot of the *Color Purple* is a bit shaky. At times it rattles around like an old car about to expire, but it is also a book that made me cry on the first page, that I could read again and again and I don't need to because it has lived with me ever since I read it. The plot flaws simply reveal what we know already: a great writer can take you anywhere and Alice Walker took me by the hand in the first hundred words and didn't let go. Would I give *The Color Purple* five stars even though I have reservations about the actual story? In a heartbeat – it deserves no less.

3. That brings me on to Amazon's star rating. Five doesn't mean it is one of the best books ever written. It means you loved it, which is rather different. Four stars say you liked it while three damns it with faint praise by saying it was ok. (And a book that arouses no strong feelings is a sad book.) Two stars reveal active dislike and one star should be reserved for those books you hate. If you give a book four stars you might want to say why it missed out on five.

4. Reviewing doesn't need to draw blood – trust me, being given one or two stars hurts enough. However, you have a right and responsibility to write an honest review.

Non-fiction
Probably the most important questions to answer when you are considering non-fiction is:

1. What did the author set out to do?
2. How well did they do it?

You could review *Back to Creative Writing School* right now because no thinking time is needed and no research required – you've already done the work. I would also appreciate a review. No, that's not quite true. I would love you to take the time and trouble to submit a review to Amazon or anywhere else you can. That direct feedback from readers means a lot, but I'm not asking for any favours – see point 4 above.

For this particular book you might like to consider:

END OF YEAR ASSESSMENT

Did you do any of the exercises?
Did you enjoy doing them? Why? Why not?
Was your imagination stretched in new and unexpected directions?
Was the author's tone (ok, *my* tone) engaging or off putting? Did I fire you with enthusiasm or crush your spirit?
Has it helped you on your journey to become the writer you want to be?

What not to include
If you bought a washing machine it would be appropriate to mention customer service, but in a book review you need to focus on the content. The following extract comes from a 44 word Amazon review of Mark Twain's *Huckleberry Finn*. It's a good example of what not to do.

- Item arrived immediately and was as described.
- This was a free electronic book so you can't go wrong.
- Thought I'd try another free classic.

Yes, yes, but what was it like? Half of the review wasted on things I really do not need to know. After that I don't care what he or she says about the book because I've already decided that we don't get on and I would probably not join the reviewer for a drink even if he or she were buying. (The older I get the more often I find myself applying this test.)

One more thing about submitting an online review or, indeed, an online anything.
Nothing falls through the (inter)net. It catches what you write and doesn't let go. As you can never predict when your words will float to the surface, don't post a review that you would be ashamed to acknowledge if Steven Spielberg was negotiating for the film rights of your first novel.

The safest thing to do is to act is if everything you write online is a postcard left by the office water cooler that will never ever be thrown away.

Last piece of advice

I've said this before, but some things are worth repeating...

Write as much as you can about anything.

Read as much as you can about anything.

Read rubbish to gain confidence and learn how not to do it. Read the books that you would reach into a fire to save. Read them first for the enjoyment, read them again because they deserve it, but also because you can now see where they went right.

Write lots. Read lots.

Write and read. That's it really.

SUGGESTED READING – A VERY PARTIAL SELECTION

Bestseller by Celia Brayfield HarperCollins (1996)
I bought it after it was recommended to me by an author who had already written a bestseller. Excellent on plot, this is much more than a how-to book. It is well-written, intelligent advice about the art of constructing a compelling story from a writer who was a bestselling novelist before she wrote it.

The Art of Fiction by David Lodge Penguin (1994)
Fifty chapters on different topics drawn from the writer's newspaper columns in the *Independent on Sunday* and the *Washington Post*, each one exploring the work of a different writer. It includes irony and Arnold Bennett, repetition and Ernest Hemingway and point of view with Henry James. Accessible and easy to dip into, it is also a lively examination of how literary devices work in real books.

Reading Like a Writer: A Guide for People Who Love Books and for Those Who Want to Write Them by Francine Prose Harper (2007)
A New York Times bestseller, I first came across this in a Chicago bookshop and it is an American version of *The Art of Fiction*, longer and perhaps more demanding, as the author wants readers to slow down and pay close attention to words and paragraphs. It is an erudite

guide to the lessons we can learn from the greats: Dostoyevsky, Flaubert, Kafka, Austen, Dickens and Le Carré among many others. It may leave you feeling that you haven't read enough and it would be true: so many books, so little time, but it may also lead you to discover writers that you might otherwise have missed.

Wannabe a Writer by Jane Wenham-Jones Accent Press (2007)
Reading this book is like having a chat with an expert in a wine bar when you decide what the hell, you'll have a whole bottle after all. It's breezy, conversational and encouraging. It covers every aspect of writing from journalism to novels, taking in rhymes for Christmas cards and television drama along the way. It includes advice on writer's bottom and how to plan using a roll of wallpaper. While its style might not appeal to everyone, I know good books that have been written as a result of the information contained in this confidence-building guide.

The Complete Artist's Way by Julia Cameron Jeremy P. Tarcher (2007)
There are now a number of books in *The Artist's Way* series – the first was published in 1992 – including one for parents who want to encourage their children to be creative. A teacher, author, artist, poet, playwright, journalist and filmmaker, Julia was briefly married to film director Martin Scorsese in the 1970s.

Creative Writing: A Practical Guide by Julia Casterton Palgrave Macmillan (3rd edition 2005)
This book has gone into three editions because of its depth and its width. It tackles some subjects that are usually ignored such as writing just for yourself and preparing your poems for performance. I never knew Julia when she taught poetry at City Lit, but I do know that she was an inspiration to many students.

Writing Down the Bones by Natalie Goldberg Shambhala Publications Inc (2005)
An international bestseller, a review described it as writing as spiritual practice and I must admit that might have put me off if I read it before I bought it. I'm sure that Nathalie's approach is informed by the Zen meditation she has been practicing much of her life, but it is not something she parades. This is for anyone who is not sure if they

are good enough or for those who have forgotten why they wanted to write in the first place. It's a gulp of oxygen at 15,000 feet.

The Ode Less Travelled: Unlocking the Poet Within by Stephen Fry (Hutchinson 2005)
Most poetry guides I've seen seem to assume a certain amount of prior knowledge: Fry doesn't. He believes if you can read and write and speak English, you can write poetry. But his focus is on the traditional rules and tools that poets employ – this book is not for you if you are only interested in writing free verse. By the time you have gone through all his exercises he promises/threatens that you will be able to write a Petrarchan sonnet, a Sapphic ode and a villanelle.

On Writing by Stephen King Hodder (2001)
Term after term students told me that this was the reason they had enrolled in a creative writing class. I'm not sure what I expected, but probably not something as gripping as this. It is part autobiography and part a tough-love guide for novelists and in both King displays his extraordinary story-telling skills. He is candid about his addictions and the devils that torment him and equally frank about the seminal role his wife has played in his success. It was she who pulled the manuscript of *Carrie* out of the trash and encouraged him to revise it.

Short Circuit: A Guide to the Art of the Short Story edited by Vanessa Gebbie Salt Publishing (2nd Edition 2013)
This collection of 24 essays is essential reading for short story writers – there is nothing else quite like it on the market. Learn the craft of short fiction from experienced and prize-winning short story writers. They share favourite exercises and favourite stories and explain their approach to writing. The advice is sometimes contradictory, but I never did believe that one size fits all.

Printed in Great Britain
by Amazon

16445775R00090